GOSPELSICK

RYAN PORTER MD
GOSPELSICK

A Missionary Doctor's Prescription for Church Revival

Plano, Texas

Gospelsick
A Missionary Doctor's Prescription for Church Revival
Copyright © 2024 by Ryan Porter

All rights reserved.

No part of this work may be reproduced or transmitted in any form or by any means, electronic or mechanical, including photocopying and recording, or by any information storage or retrieval system, except as may be expressly permitted by the 1976 Copyright Act or in writing from the publisher. Requests for permission can be addressed to Permissions, Invite Press, P.O. Box 260917, Plano, TX 75026.

This book is printed on acid-free, elemental chlorine-free paper.

Paperback: 9781963265101; eBook: 9781963265118

All scripture quotations, unless noted otherwise, are taken from THE HOLY BIBLE, NEW INTERNATIONAL VERSION®, NIV® Copyright © 1973, 1978, 1984, 2011 by Biblica, Inc.™ Used by permission of Zondervan. All rights reserved worldwide.

24 25 26 27 28 29 30 31 32 33—10 9 8 7 6 5 4 3 2 1

MANUFACTURED in the UNITED STATES of AMERICA

Contents

Introduction   vii

Chapter One: What Is Gospel Deficiency?   1

Chapter Two: Body Odor, or What's That Smell?   17

Chapter Three: Pica   29

Chapter Four: Myopia   39

Chapter Five: Impotence   53

Chapter Six: Expressive Aphasia   67

Chapter Seven: Excising Barriers   81

Chapter Eight: Autoimmune Disorder   103

Chapter Nine: Remission   117

Chapter Ten: Prevention   127

Chapter Eleven: Gospel Sufficiency   135

Endnotes   141

Introduction

When the customs and border agent stamped our passports and said, "Welcome home," we didn't realize how un-home-like it would feel to exit the airport. Despite living most of our lives in America, it suddenly felt like a foreign country. This was our first time back in the United States since starting our new life as medical missionaries living in West Africa. By that time, we had only been away for two years, but it felt like a lifetime. Driving down the highway, seeing once-familiar places felt more like lucid dreaming, being awake and in a dream at the same time. It's hard to describe reverse culture shock to someone who has never experienced it, but if you have, you understand.

It was the same in many ways, seeing familiar faces. We visited friends and family, former churches, and old Bible study groups, and it was wonderful to see everyone. But in many interactions, it was clear that something had changed. It felt as though we had been asleep for two years and had just woken up. Everything had changed, yet we were frozen in time from when we had left home.

The biggest change we noticed was the content of conversations, which displayed diminished joy and heightened anxiety or even outright anger. People seemed more critical and suspicious of each other. Conversations quickly turned from simple catching up to complaining about current events or the state of the country.

To be fair, a lot had happened during the time we were away. We departed America just a few weeks before COVID-19 caused everything to shut down. Shortly after we arrived in a new country with a new language and culture, the borders and airports closed, preventing us from leaving even if we wanted to. (We didn't want to, but it's nice to have the option.) We like to say that God opened all the doors to move us overseas and then slammed the door shut behind us. Back in America, in addition to COVID, there were protests, riots, and gun and racial violence—all during a major election year.

Interestingly, as we witnessed firsthand how polarized our passport country had become, we observed another surreal pattern: people projected their personal, polarized perspectives on us. Since we were frozen in time from an American culture standpoint, everyone assumed we felt the same way as they did. We were a blank canvas for them, on which they could paint their own self-reflections and ideals. For those we left behind, it was as though everyone had picked a side in some cosmic, existential tug of war. Since we were absent when the teams were chosen, everyone presumed we were on their side.

Our new home in Africa, where we still live today, does not have the greatest internet access, so despite being generally aware of these topical issues, we certainly were not up to date on all the drama and details. This left us doing a lot of silent nodding during conversations and subsequent googling afterward to find out why people were talking about injecting bleach or dead people voting beyond the grave.

This made for a fascinating view of the state of the union in general and American Christianity in particular. All of this polarization, fear, and quarreling had infiltrated the Church as well. In some cases, the Church even spearheaded it. Families that used to hang out together and do Bible studies together were now disparaging each other. They had picked different teams. To them, their (former) friend was now an enemy.

Some of this was division over who got vaccinated or not, who sheltered in place or not, who voted for whom, and who thinks which lives matter. Throughout these conversations, my wife and I decided not to volunteer our personal opinions for a few reasons. One, because we were less informed and, in some cases, did not feel as strongly or as angrily as many did. Two, because that was not the purpose of our visit. But third, and most of all, because it wasn't the most important thing to talk about. We wanted to talk about the gospel spreading in an unreached country and how God was working around the world. But for some reason, this wasn't a captivating conversation topic for many people.

Clearly, something was going on. Something had changed. Priorities had shifted. Or maybe true priorities and interests were just finally coming to the surface. Maybe all of the polarization, outrage, and fear was always there, but people were simply better able or willing to manage it. Either way, the cat was out of the bag, lines were drawn, sides were picked, and none of this had to do with the gospel. The life-saving, world-changing message for which we left comfort and country to spread around the world seemed to have taken a backseat to worldly pursuits and interests. The war for the kingdom of God and the very souls of every human being fell to a distant second behind the newly prioritized culture wars.

Since this experience, it has become abundantly clear to me that this is not just a situational reaction to extreme circumstances. This is not just about people who were quarantined for too long acting out. It's not just a phase or a short-lived trend like parachute pants or late-'90s swing music. What we are witnessing in the American Church today is a full-on disease. It is a sickness that is more contagious and more deadly than COVID and smallpox combined.

Unfortunately, the vast majority of those infected don't have any idea they are ill. The signs and symptoms have perniciously grown and spread slowly enough that they have gone unnoticed by most. Certainly, the effects of the disease are being felt and the symptoms are manifesting in various ways within the Church, but even so, the condition I'm describing remains largely undiagnosed.

So, what is it? What is this mysterious, metastatic malady with massive morbidity and mortality? I call it *Gospel Deficiency*, a newly defined/made-up diagnosis to describe a troubling condition affecting Christians all over the world. It is infiltrative and corruptive to the Christian's soul and directly affects every single person around us. Unfortunately, its signs and symptoms have become so ubiquitous in the Church that, at best, we have largely accepted that this is the way things are, and at worst, we preach that this is the way things should be.

Simply put, Gospel Deficiency is a condition wherein the gospel of Jesus Christ, the good news of his death and resurrection, has little impact and influence on how Christians live, think, act, and view others. This deficit leads to an anemic form of Christianity that is embodied by a large number of American Evangelicals and has come to define the faith in the eyes of the outside world. And rather than recognize and remedy the problem directly, we grasp at the straw-like things of the world like politics, social reform, programs, and various efforts at relevance that have no power to save us or others.

On top of our own souls wasting away because of this spiritual scourge, the world around us is suffering as well. The gospel is the greatest need the world has, because it is the only thing by which people can be saved (Acts 4:12). But despite this, our deficiency of explicit gospel witness means that billions of people will continue to live and die apart from Christ. The very thing that saves us and has the power to save the world (Romans 1:16) is being withheld by the very ones who were entrusted with its dissemination.

In short, our friends, family, neighbors, coworkers, and everyone else who is living far from God is suffering from a terminal illness—an illness for which we know the cure—and yet, we not only fail to offer it, but often actively refuse. Without correction, this shortcoming forsakes our God-given mandate to bless the nations and will be the very thing that leads to the failure of our churches, as we fail to obey our King's mandated commission (Matthew 28:18–20).

This is the plague of Gospel Deficiency in our day. It is not new to our time, but it continues to spread largely unhindered in our modern Christian culture as we prioritize the things and issues of this world over and above the gospel. The goal of this book is not to comment on how to think about those worldly issues but to highlight the need to elevate the gospel above all those issues and to see the gospel take its rightful place in our lives as *the* issue we are most passionate about and about which we want to convince people.

Over the last several years of living in Africa, I've had a unique vantage point from which to see Gospel Deficiency continue to develop in my passport country of America. This distance and the exposure to new cultures helped crystallize what I initially observed as a collection of symptoms into a definable diagnosis. Living in a foreign culture can help you look at your own culture objectively in a way that you can't when you're inside it. Moreover, moving from a Christian-majority context to a country that is less than 1 percent Christian has a way of lending a new perspective—namely, an eternal perspective—and an urgency to spread the gospel.

As a medical doctor, I am approaching Gospel Deficiency as I would a medical disease. Therefore, this book will follow the outline of a traditional doctor's assessment. I'll start with the "history of present illness" to define and describe the state of the problem and how it manifests. Chapters 2 through 8 will each focus on a symptom, including diagnostics to determine the presence and state of affliction, followed by recommendations for treatment. The concluding chapters will look at approaches to staying in remission after treatment and preventing recurrence while embracing a gospel-sufficient life.

In many parts of the world (though thankfully not all), the Church has been wasting away for decades, most noticeably in the West, and is now in critical condition. However, I, for one, am not ready to call time of death on the modern evangelical church. Yes, we see waning numbers and influence and severe systemic issues, but none of these are a death sentence. Like an electrolyte deficiency, Gospel Deficiency can range in severity from needing just a little tune-up to severe depletion, leading to full-on cardiac arrest. Whatever level of severity, the purpose of this book is to help us all diagnose this deficiency within ourselves and our churches while offering treatment recommendations and hope for a gospel-filled future.

Just as Christ healed the sick and raised the dead, He alone has the power to revive this particular heart condition. He has given us His Holy Spirit to lead us and guide us and give us all that we need. He is able to fill our gospel tanks so that we can live into the abundant gospel life He has for us. For the sake of the kingdom of God and the billions of spiritual captives around the world, may it be so. Amen.

Chapter One
What Is Gospel Deficiency?

Code stat. I dropped my sandwich and ran for the stairs. These two words make any doctor's heart sink. Particularly when you are, as I was at the time, a resident in training who is on call and responsible for responding to the code and managing the situation. Not only was the overhead announcement played all over the hospital, it was loud and abrupt like an unwelcome alarm early in the morning. There may as well have been electrodes attached to my chair to shock me out of complacency, providing a jolt of literal energy.

As I exited the stairwell, I hurried to the room swarming with the commotion of crying family members in the hallway and diligent nurses rushing about. No matter how many times you've seen similar situations on TV, nothing can prepare you for the reality. On TV, the actor-doctors may as well be tickling the chest of the "dying patient." In reality, you feel ribs breaking beneath your palms with every life-sustaining chest compression. On TV, the patient usually survives. In reality, only a fraction of patients who suffer cardiac arrest leave the hospital through the front door.

"What's the story?" The patient's nurse gave me a quick summary of events leading up to his heart stopping. He just arrived in the emergency department with his family due to persistent nausea, vomiting, and lethargy. He was increasingly confused and eventually became unresponsive with rapid breathing just before his heart monitor flatlined.

As the response team continued chest compressions, another nurse ran in with his bloodwork results, the paper still warm from the printer. The results told me that his blood had turned to acid, his kidneys were failing, and his blood sugar was off the chart.

"What does he take for his diabetes?" I asked. "He doesn't have diabetes," came the response. In an instant, the curtain dropped, revealing the diagnosis and cause of his current state. All of his issues, from the preceding symptoms to his current critical condition, stemmed from undiagnosed, untreated diabetes. His body lacked the insulin necessary to maintain basic organ function, a life-threatening deficiency that, when left untreated, all but guarantees your very own *code stat*.

[Insert record stopping sound effect.] Hold up. Isn't this supposed to be a Christian living book (or whatever you call it), not an episode of *[insert popular medical drama]*? Fair enough. But hey, why not a little bit of both?

Just like this patient was in critical condition because of a severe deficiency of insulin, there is an even more serious deficiency affecting many Christians in America and other countries around the world: Gospel Deficiency. And just like our diabetic patient certainly had warning signs and symptoms long before his heart stopped, my hope in this book is to help readers identify this problem, recognize the warning signs, and suggest a pathway to turning things around before it is too late. But before we get into what it means to have a *deficiency*, let's take a quick look at *gospel*.

We Have Some Good News

The gospel is a fascinating thing. We use the word *gospel* all the time as if it is a simplistic, one-dimensional thing, even though we may not all agree on its definition. For Paul and the New Testament writers, the gospel was dynamic and multifaceted. It was news about an event of the past while at the same time a window into the future. It was taken around the world by Christ followers while at the same time going forth in its own dynamic power. It illuminates the pathway of salvation while at the same time warning of coming condemnation.

Nowadays, *gospel* is often used to include anything and everything Christians do and teach. Some might say going to work and being a good person is "living out the gospel." Others might contend that serving food at a homeless shelter is "gospel work." For our purposes, we will use *gospel* to refer to the good news to be proclaimed that, as Paul explains it, "Christ died for our sins according to the Scriptures, that he was buried, that he was raised on the third day according to the Scriptures" (1 Corinthians 15:3–4). Paul calls this message, which he received and passed on to others all around the world, "of first importance." He lived out this priority designation by making the gospel message the first and primary focus of his interactions in all the towns and villages he visited. Where he went, the gospel went and was heard.

In addition to the gospel as good news of a past event, the gospel also points forward to a future good news: God's kingdom coming in fullness in the new creation (Revelation 21) as a direct result of this past event. This future good news is what we look forward to. It gives us hope for eternal communion with our loving creator and the eventual destruction of evil and suffering.

As we live in the intermission between Christ's first and second coming, between the past and future good news events, we have the privilege to glorify the King by living into the fullness of the gospel and announcing this good news to others. And as we will see, since the beginning of the Church, this has been the norm and expectation for all Christians.

By this definition of "gospel" as a specific, glorious, life-changing message of good news, it is something to be communicated wherein the events and ramifications of Christ's death, burial, resurrection, and Lordship are made explicit. It is a message that all Christians at some point received and believed when we decided to follow Christ. And it is this message that our King commissioned us to preach to the perishing whose minds have been blinded by Satan (2 Corinthians 4:4).

Defining Gospel Deficiency

If the gospel is the good news that we accept and share with others, then what does it mean to be gospel deficient? A deficiency implies that the level or amount of *something* is lower than it should be, and that decreased amount leads to unfavorable conditions. So, if we suffer from Gospel Deficiency, this implies that the presence and impact of the gospel is minimized in our life so as to not have the appropriate effect, resulting in an unhealthy state of being.

To say the gospel is minimized or not having the appropriate effect in one's life is still vague, so let's flesh it out. Anyone who is a follower of Christ, at one point in their life, heard this good news and responded to it by submitting to Jesus as Lord of their life. If Jesus is truly Lord of our life, we have the Holy Spirit with us continually working in us and through us and filling us with Christ-like love for others. Unfortunately, we often inhibit this process through our own fallenness and sin and un-Christ-like selfish desires. This self-inflicted inhibition of our sanctification minimizes the presence and effect of the gospel in our lives. That's Gospel Deficiency: the inhibition or minimization of the gospel in our life diminishing its internal effects in us and our proclamation of it to others.

The Christian life is meant to be characterized and defined by the gospel. That is to say, the Christian life should be gospel shaped. When people interact with us, they should see and receive the testimony of the good news of Christ. Everything we do and think and say should be a testimony to the love of Christ defined by His self-sacrificial submission to the cross. But when the gospel becomes deficient in us, the shape of our life becomes distorted and our gospel proclamation fades away. Like a wheel losing its round shape is unable to serve its intended purpose, so is a Christian life that loses its distinct gospel shape.

In addition to something other than the love of Christ driving our present thoughts and actions, Gospel Deficiency is defined by losing sight of that future good news. It is a lack of eternal perspective. When the gospel is fully manifest in our lives, we begin to see the present through the lens of the future. We have the promise of eternity with our Savior to look forward to. That means that this momentary life is but a fleeting blip in the light of eternity. Therefore, insofar as the concerns of this world do not have an eternal impact, they should fall down our prioritized list of concerns behind those that do have eternal relevance.

Paul tells the Colossians, "Since, then, you have been raised with Christ, set your hearts on things above, where Christ is, seated at the right hand of God. Set your minds on things above, not on earthly things. For you died, and your life is now hidden with Christ in God" (Colossians 3:1–3). He also tells the Corinthians,

"If anyone is in Christ, the new creation has come: The old has gone, the new is here!" (2 Corinthians 5:17). If we have truly died to this world (Galatians 2:20) and are a new creation in Christ, then our minds are fixed, not on earthly things, but on the eternal "things above."

This eternal perspective does not just affect how we think about our own life and the fleeting nature of things such as work, money, and status (which is how an eternal perspective is typically preached). Living in light of eternity and setting our minds on things above affects and redefines how we view others. Rather than seeing people from a worldly point of view as mere neighbors, coworkers, or political opponents, we see them as people to whom Christ has ascribed unsurpassable worth by dying for them on the cross. A gospel-shaped life lived in the light of eternity will see those living far from God as blinded, bound captives in need of a Savior.

However, this perspective short-circuits in a gospel-deficient life. This may lead one to increasingly view things as the world does. We begin to look at others not through the lens of the cross, but through the lens of our flesh and selfish desires. Those who, from an eternal perspective, are captives in need of a Savior are reduced to mere friends or acquaintances or other designations that are defined in relation to self rather than in relation to the Father.

A Heart Condition

Gospel Deficiency, at its root, is really a heart condition characterized by a loss of love. Jesus tells us the first and greatest commandment is to love the Lord your God with all your heart, soul, mind, and strength. And the second is to love your neighbor (Matthew 23:37–39). So how do we love God and love others, and what does that have to do with the gospel?

Among other answers, if you ask a group of Christians how to love God, someone is likely to say we should follow His commands. Jesus tells us as much in John 14:15 when he says, "If you love me, keep my commands." That's pretty direct and to the point. Eventually, if you wait long enough, someone in the group will say, albeit begrudgingly perhaps, we love God by telling others about him. Not only does this make intuitive sense (after all, a husband who doesn't want to tell others about his wife would be a bit suspect), but it is also a command that we share the gospel with others.

We can see how sharing the gospel is an expression of love for God, but what about loving others? Far too many people, Christians and non-Christians alike, have seen forms of evangelism that were less than ideal. Even saying the dreaded "E-word" might make you sick to your stomach if you have been on the wrong end of hurtful evangelism. This may bring to mind scenarios like angry preachers on the street corner telling passersby that they are going to hell, or smooth-talking televangelists who offer salvation and blessing for the low cost of $49.99 a month. Private jets aren't cheap, after all!

The truth is, we don't tend to think about evangelism in terms of loving people well. If you were on *Family Feud* and they surveyed 100 Christians and asked them, "How can we best love people?," I doubt sharing the gospel would even make it up on Steve Harvey's big board, let alone be near the top. Stop for a moment and think about how you would answer that question.

We tend to think about loving people well through ministries like feeding the hungry, mission trips, clothes closets, and medical clinics for low-income families. Maybe we think about visiting sick church members in the hospital or mowing the yard for homebound people. No doubt these are all excellent ways to love people, and we should absolutely continue doing these things. I am thankful for the many servant-hearted Christians who care for people through ministries like these.

However, I submit that sharing the gospel should not only be on this list but should be at the very top. Think about it: What more loving thing could you do for a person than introduce them to their Savior? To invite them into God's family so that they too can become a reconciled, righteous, new creation (2 Corinthians 5:17–20)? To show them what it means to follow Jesus and inherit eternal life? This is without question the most loving thing we can do for people who are far from God. No amount of meals, clothes, or service projects can compare to the gift of eternal life.

Not only is sharing the gospel the most loving service we can offer someone, but to take it one step further, if we are not sharing the gospel, can we really say we are loving people the way in which we are commanded? If "love others" is the second greatest commandment and sharing the gospel is the ultimate expression of fulfilling this commandment, how can we claim to truly love others, especially the lost, if our interactions with them are devoid of the gospel message?

All this is *not* to say that anyone who doesn't share the gospel with everyone they know is devoid of love. Certainly, evangelism is not the only expression of love, even if it is the greatest. Many Christians are really good at loving people. The truth is, we *are* really good at loving people—the way *we* want to love them. Our expressions of love for others often come in the forms that we think are best or maybe the forms that most fit our natural predilections or gifting.

For example, hospitality can be a wonderful expression of love. It is also a distinct gift that some people have. Those predisposed to or gifted in hospitality may be more prone to express love this way because it comes naturally to them and likely brings them joy. Likewise, those who are more naturally servant-hearted will veer toward opportunities to love people through acts of service.

I certainly don't want to diminish these or any other biblical expression of Christ-like love. What I do want, and this will be a recurring theme in this book, is to see the gospel and evangelism elevated to its proper place in daily Christian life and discourse. For far too long, sharing the gospel has been relegated to something that is optional or programmed or left to those with the gift of evangelism. As we will see, this is an unbiblical view and practice of evangelism, not to mention a disservice to the King and His bride, the Church.

Just as we are good at loving people how we want to love them, we are equally good at rationalizing reasons not to love people in the ways in which we do not want to love them. Maybe you have even started to do this as you are reading: "I'm not gifted in evangelism." "I don't know what to say." "What if they ask me a questions I can't answer?" "I don't have a close enough relationship with them to share the gospel." These are all common responses to teachings about evangelism. Fortunately, none of these barriers, which we will discuss in a later chapter, are insurmountable.

Gospel Compassion

In addition to seeing gospel proclamation in terms of love for others, we also must learn to see it as a form of compassion. Oftentimes the term *compassion ministries* is used to refer to programs that serve the tangible needs of those who are lacking basic necessities such as medicine, food, and shelter. But as we will see, evangelism is a ministry of compassion.

Jesus went through all the towns and villages, teaching in their synagogues, proclaiming the good news of the kingdom and healing every disease and sickness. When he saw the crowds, he had *compassion* on them, because they were harassed and helpless, like sheep without a shepherd. Then he said to his disciples, "The harvest is plentiful but the workers are few. Ask the Lord of the harvest, therefore, to send out workers into his harvest field." Jesus called his twelve disciples to him . . . . These twelve Jesus sent out [to proclaim the kingdom]. (Matthew 9:35–10:7, emphasis added)

This passage starts with verse 35 giving a quick fast-forward summary of Jesus' ministry of proclaiming the kingdom throughout several places. This verse transitions the story from the preceding verses to set the stage for what follows. It's the biblical equivalent of a musical montage in a movie that moves the story forward in a summative fashion.

Verse 36 shows Jesus surrounded by a large crowd, which Matthew describes as "harassed and helpless like sheep without a shepherd." As a point of clarity, the word *harassed* also can be translated as "distressed," which better communicates the intended meaning to American ears, since "harassed" may connote the idea of being attacked or bothered by someone (although, from a spiritual warfare stance, that could also be true). Matthew then compares the distressed, helpless masses to "sheep without a shepherd." What does it mean to compare the lost to sheep without a shepherd?

When we first moved to Africa, my wife and I had no experience with sheep or any other livestock. Despite growing up in Texas, I knew nothing about cattle or horses or any other farm animals, nor did I have any desire to. Like Sherlock Holmes said—and I agree—"They're dangerous at both ends and crafty in the middle."[1] But in Africa, cows, sheep, donkeys, and all other sorts of animals are everywhere. Prior to that, I had never witnessed sheep behavior firsthand. When sheep are with their shepherd, they all stick together and follow where he leads. It's not uncommon for us to see a single shepherd, sometimes even a child, walking along with 100 sheep right behind him. The shepherd leads and the sheep follow.

Sheep without a shepherd, on the other hand, are a completely different animal. They are aimless. They putter around only seeking to fill their stomachs with whatever they can find. They are skittish and startle easily, running away from the smallest sound or disturbance.

Despite my aversion to farm animals, it is hard not to have compassion for these wandering, shepherd-less sheep. One day, I saw a young sheep get separated from his shepherd. I could see the flock grazing on the other side of the road behind some trees, but this little guy couldn't see them. He proceeded to run circles around the house over and over, crying and searching. He must have lapped that house five times, each time undoubtedly thinking, *Maybe* this *will be the time I find them!* It was heartbreaking. I knew I needed to point him toward his shepherd. I walked toward him to try to help guide him back to the flock, but he just ran away from me, scared. He didn't know who to trust, so he wouldn't let me help him. Such is the state of a distressed, helpless sheep without a shepherd.

When Jesus saw the crowds as if they were sheep without a shepherd, "he had compassion on them." He saw their plight, saw their suffering, saw their need for a shepherd, and therefore engaged their need out of love. He knew that He alone could satisfy the deepest longings of their souls and was moved to compassion.

Often when we see sheep without a shepherd, meaning those who are not following Jesus, we see their suffering or the suffering they cause others, and we are quick to blame them for their station in life. When they act like what they are, non-Christians, we may automatically view them as bad people, or think that they should know better, or condemn them for not acting like Christians (of course, why would they if they are not Christians?).

I picture myself watching Jesus interacting compassionately with different crowds. For example, in the narrative of him feeding the 4,000, Matthew 15:32 quotes Jesus saying he had compassion on the people who had been with him three days and had nothing to eat. My fallen, judgmental spirit thinks, *Why would they be out there for three days, far from home, and not think about bringing a sack lunch? Once they saw how far they were going, shouldn't they have had the forethought to prepare or turn back? What kind of parent would bring their kids way out here without a way to feed them? I might need to call Child Protective Services. That lady carrying a baby must be a bad mom to let that child wear the same poopy diaper for this long. She should have brought her diaper bag.* My fallen, judgmental spirit could go on, but you get the point.

Fortunately, Jesus isn't like me. Back in Matthew 9:36, it says that He saw them and had compassion on them. And how does His compassion manifest in this passage? He basically saw the large number of lost people and said to His disciples in verses 37 and 38, "Guys, it's going to take a lot of workers to help these people and share the gospel with everyone. Until they hear the good news of the kingdom and follow me, they are going to continue to live as sheep without a shepherd."

This passage marks the end of Matthew 9, but remember that the original author did not put in the chapter breaks. Those were put in later. And while usually quite helpful, these chapter breaks occasionally make one, unified teaching look like two separate stories, which muddies the waters.

Immediately following these verses at end of chapter 9, without a break in the story, Jesus gathered His disciples and sent them out to proclaim the gospel. He sent them out into the harvest to various towns and villages to continue spreading the good news of the kingdom. Jesus' compassion for the lost led directly to proclaiming the gospel to them. We see that Jesus also commanded His disciples to cast out demons, heal the sick, and raise the dead as they went for the primary purpose of proclaiming the arrival of the kingdom.

For us, we see sheep without a shepherd every day. Whether at work or school or on TV or social media, we see lost people all the time. Maybe we see them make bad choices that lead to bad consequences. Our fallen reaction might think, *Well, he should have known better, and he got what he deserved.* Maybe we see people pushing a political ideology that we find reprehensible, which then spills over into us finding *them* reprehensible rather than viewing them with compassion as distressed, helpless sheep without a shepherd. Next time you scroll through social media or read the news, listen to your internal monologue, and you may catch yourself gravitating toward a judgmental, fallen reaction to the lost rather than a compassionate, loving, Christ-like response. That's Gospel Deficiency.

Jesus sees sheep without a shepherd, has compassion, and says, "How can I help guide them to their shepherd?" He knows that the outward behavior and bad decisions that lost sheep make are just the symptoms, not the disease. He goes straight to the heart of the issue with surgical precision to offer the definitive cure of His saving grace.

We spend a lot of our time and emotional energy focused on the symptoms. We want to fix people's behavior or enact laws to stop them from making bad decisions. However, the root issue, the eternal issue, the issue that Christ calls us to engage is the issue of the lost sheep not having a shepherd. The gospel of Jesus Christ is the greatest need of all people in all places for all time. Proclaiming the gospel is the only means we are given and commanded to use to help those who are lost and dying without the gospel. A failure to recognize this stems from Gospel Deficiency that must be rectified.

The gospel is love. The gospel is compassion. Living it and sharing it with others is a privilege and a duty. We miss out on experiencing the fullness of God's love and compassion and power when we let our gospel tanks run dry. And the people around us who are in need of a shepherd miss out on hearing and seeing the path to salvation.

Conclusion

Today we see that Gospel Deficiency has become widespread in the Western Church. Unfortunately, it is a plague to which none are immune. Its ubiquity highlights our urgent need for a clear diagnosis and treatment plan to be developed. So how can we tell if we are affected? What are some of the signs and symptoms one might exhibit under the influence of the disease?

A church that had similar issues in a somewhat similar setting was the church at Corinth. In Paul's letters to the Corinthians, particularly 2 Corinthians, Paul responds to and corrects them on several points related to, what I am calling, their Gospel Deficiency.

In 2 Corinthians, Paul is speaking to his strained relationship with the Corinthians. This tension was not due simply to a theological disagreement between Paul and the church, but was rooted in a clash between Corinthian cultural values and the Christian values Paul wanted them to adopt. In this, they had begun prioritizing a worldly way of thinking while drifting away from the gospel that Paul preached to them. The correspondence reveals that this community of relatively new believers was not embracing their new identity by living out the gospel-shaped life, so Paul was calling them back to the centrality of Christ crucified.[2]

Corinth was a busy city and served as a popular destination for travelers, tourists, and business people. It had a vibrant economy that also attracted immigrants from all over the world, thus creating a bit of a "melting pot" atmosphere. This led to a church filled with people of diverse backgrounds and social standing. Sound familiar? It had a lot in common with the United States, so it serves as a good point of comparison.

To elucidate the symptoms of Gospel Deficiency, we will use 2 Corinthians as a case study. We will compare several characteristics of a gospel-shaped life with the corresponding symptoms of a gospel-deficient life. Examining these issues faced by the Corinthians and how Paul addressed them will help us to better understand and address our modern equivalents.

In medicine, we look at a patient's history and symptoms as well as objective measures like lab tests in order to make a definitive diagnosis and treatment recommendations. As we approach Gospel Deficiency as a disease to be diagnosed and treated, we will look at it through this lens of a medical assessment. The next several chapters will each cover one aspect, or symptom, of Gospel Deficiency, followed by self-assessment and diagnostic questions, and ending with treatment recommendations. Though several additional symptoms could be added, particular emphasis is given to symptoms affecting three aspects of our spiritual lives: our personal relationship with Christ, our view of the world and its inhabitants (particularly non-Christians), and our actions toward others particularly as they relate to sharing the gospel message. So have a seat, settle in, and let's have a look.

Chapter Two
Body Odor, or What's That Smell?

But thanks be to God, who always leads us as captives in Christ's triumphal procession and uses us to spread the aroma of the knowledge of him everywhere. (2 Corinthians 2:14)

If the ministry that brought condemnation was glorious, how much more glorious is the ministry that brings righteousness! (2 Corinthians 3:9)

During my medical training, I worked with one physician who was smart and funny and whom I really liked. The only thing I did not like was how strong his cologne was every single day. It wasn't a bad scent. It was just slap-you-in-the-face strong. You could smell it down the hall and around the corner. If I entered a new patient ward where he was working, I could smell his presence even before seeing him. Everyone could. But God love him, he was dedicated to that scent and wouldn't change it, or the amount he wore, no matter what people said about it.

Likewise, a gospel-shaped life spreads the aroma of the knowledge of God everywhere; that is, it spreads the good news of Jesus Christ. As with my former colleague, when our life is defined by the love of our Savior, that loving scent is strong enough to be sensed by everyone around us.

It is important to note at the outset that we are not the source of the aroma, but it comes from the presence of Christ in us. Our role is to spread the aroma (or, more accurately, be "used" by God to spread the aroma), not determine whether people accept it. The gospel is good news, so if our scent is coming from the message of Christ, it will be inherently sweet.

The problem comes not when some people inevitably do not find the gospel appealing (2 Corinthians 2:16), but when this sweet, saving scent is absent or covered up in our lives by other, let's say, stinkier things. So what type of scent are we spreading around the world? Do non-Christians today smell the sweet gospel aroma when we are near them? Do they describe Christians as those who reflect the character of Christ? You probably already know the answer, but let's look at some data.

What's That Smell?

According to a 2023 Barna study, among people who self-identify as "non-Christian," 44 percent say that local churches in their area are most known for things they are against, with only 9 percent expressing a positive view of evangelicals.[3] In fact, the number one answer for "What causes you to doubt Christianity?" was the perceived hypocrisy of Christians. Likewise, people of self-reported "no faith" selected "judgmental" as the characteristic that best describes Christians.

On the flip side, a large portion of non-Christian Americans, including 40 percent of those with "no faith," have a positive view of Jesus and His character. They noted attributes of Jesus such as caring, compassionate, and forgiving as being important to them. Even if their knowledge of Jesus is incomplete, these people recognize a disconnect between their perceptions or experience of American Christianity and what they do know about Jesus.

This research found that Christ, and at least some of His message, speaks to many of the population's primary spiritual desires, but it is largely those proclaiming to be followers of Christ who turn them off from Christianity. Jesus is seen as caring, compassionate, and loving, while Christians are largely viewed as judgmental hypocrites. In terms of our earlier analogy, many nonbelievers like the aroma of Christ, but that is decidedly not the scent they are smelling on us.

Let's dig a bit deeper into that specific statistic of churches and Christians being largely known for what they are against over and above being known for reflecting Christ. In a deeper analysis of the data, the "things they are against" were far and away issues like abortion, gay rights, and other hot-button political topics. I'd love to assume that this is due to the disproportionately loud voices on TV who focus on these issues, but experience tells a different tale. To be clear, in no way am I saying that these aren't important issues, but the reality is that these issues are being pushed to the forefront more than Christ Himself, who is of utmost importance. Beyond outward appearances, in some cases Christians may even put these and other issues on the throne of their heart above Christ Himself without realizing it.

So, on one hand, we have Paul saying Christians should be so consumed and characterized by the gospel that they fill the room with the scent of Christ. And on the other hand, we have our neighbors, coworkers, and peers saying pretty clearly that the Jesus aroma is nowhere to be smelled on us, or at best is significantly masked by these other things, especially things that we are against.

Chapter Two

The New Ministry of Condemnation

In 2 Corinthians 3:9, Paul distinguishes between the ministry of condemnation and the ministry that brings righteousness. In context, he is comparing the old covenant law with the new covenant in Christ. But according to the aforementioned Barna studies, it seems that the world around us today views Christianity as a ministry of condemnation, preoccupied with condemning the things we are against. Insofar as their assessment is accurate, this is a picture of Gospel Deficiency in action.

Some Christians today live as though they are called to a ministry of condemnation, and many even revel in it. They revile and vilify certain people or groups or political parties for their differing choices and opinions. While this doesn't apply to all, many evangelicals pridefully stand as the self-appointed accusers of a fallen world rather than proclaiming freedom to the accused. Those who find themselves taking on the role of accuser toward the world around us might find that their true father is not the sacrificial Lamb of heaven but the Accuser who was cast out of heaven. They may find themselves standing with the crucifiers rather than the Crucified.[4]

Some of you may be thinking that it is right and proper to call sin *sin* and condemn the ways of the world. Certainly, that is correct. The point of emphasis here is not on condemning sin itself but on how we view and treat the sinners around us, particularly the ones with whom we disagree.

A good example of what it looks like to make this clear distinction comes from the speeches in the book of Acts. Peter and the other apostles went around calling people to repentance from wrongdoing. But they don't stop there. What the apostles called people away from was never more important than what they were calling them to: a relationship with Jesus Christ. If we merely preach condemnation and behavioral change, people are no better off. Convincing someone to improve their moral standards is drastically different than calling them to turn to the Creator of the universe and bow to Him as Lord. The speeches in Acts, along with the entire New Testament ministry, aren't only interested in changing earthly behavior, but far and away they emphasize and focus on lovingly looking toward the eternal destination of the hearers. This is what it's like to have a gospel-centered view of others.

This distinction gets spelled out more tangibly when Paul is in Ephesus and discussing baptism with some of the new believers.

> [Paul] found some disciples and asked them, "Did you receive the Holy Spirit when you believed?" They answered, "No, we have not even heard that there is a Holy Spirit." So Paul asked, "Then what baptism did you receive?" "John's baptism," they replied. Paul said, "John's baptism was a baptism of repentance. He told the people to believe in the one coming after him, that is, in Jesus." On hearing this, they were baptized in the name of the Lord Jesus. When Paul placed his hands on them, the Holy Spirit came on them, and they spoke in tongues and prophesied. (Acts 19:1–6)

A few verses before this, in Acts 18:25, we see that Apollos had been teaching people in Ephesus about Christ, but "[Apollos] knew only the baptism of John." Clearly, Apollos had some accurate knowledge of the gospel. He was calling people to repentance, but his teaching was incomplete. He was calling people away from sin and even baptizing them but not fully leading them into new life, filled with the Holy Spirit.

When Paul showed up and realized this, he clarified that, though it was true that John the Baptist called people away from sin

(Mark 1:4; Acts 13:24), that was not the end of the story. There was more to it. John also pointed people to the Savior (John 3:30). As these Ephesians understood this and fully put their trust in Christ, being baptized in His name, they received the Holy Spirit.

Again, we see that what Paul was calling people away from was never as important as what he was calling them to. It's not just a call to repentance, a ministry of condemnation, but a call to be reconciled to God. In fact, *only* calling people away from sin without leading them to Christ and the fullness of life that can be found in Him alone can be more damaging than not calling them to repentance at all. This is evidenced in the Barna studies that reveal that modern-day Christians in America are known for promoting condemnation and repentance only without the accompanying saving gospel of grace. This not only leaves people in the preexisting Savior-separated state, but it often hardens people toward God even more.

A ministry of condemnation only brings death. In Christ, through the Spirit, we have been given a ministry of righteousness and reconciliation. If we are more vocal about the things we condemn than we are in proclaiming the gospel, it's no wonder the "no faith" people remain in that category. However, if we live into our God-given ministry of reconciliation—that is, a ministry focused on reconciling people to God in Christ—that would more likely captivate the hearts of the lost. Condemnation separates; reconciliation captivates.

Rather than condemning those we label as sinful or bad, let us take up the ministry of righteousness and reconciliation, that we would strive to see those "sinful, bad" people reconciled to their Creator through Christ and thereby inherit His righteousness as they become new creations. In this, we align our heart with that of our Father's, who, as John 3:17 tells us, "did not send his Son into the world to condemn the world, but to save the world through him."

God wills that all might be saved (1 Timothy 2:4), and He sent His son for this purpose. He seeks reconciliation, not condemnation. If the all-holy, righteous, perfect God of the universe seeks salvation of sinners over condemnation, how can we put ourselves above God and think that it is our place to condemn the world? John 3:18 goes on to say, "Whoever believes in him is not condemned, but whoever does not believe stands condemned already because they have not believed in the name of God's one and only Son." For those who reject Christ, condemnation has already come, not by us, but by the very Word of God. Setting ourselves up as the moral guardians of a fallen society, clinging to a ministry of condemnation, is a hallmark sign of Gospel Deficiency that drowns out the sweet aroma of Christ in those who bear His name.

Diagnostics: The Whiff Test

What scent is your church giving off? Go undercover and ask around your community what they know about your church or what your church is known for. Based on your reconnaissance, is it one of the following?

A) A distinctly Christ-like scent

B) A good scent but not distinctly Christ-like

C) A bad scent

D) No scent at all—they don't even know you're there

Chapter Two

Ask your friends, family, and coworkers what scent they smell on you; make sure you ask people who will be brutally honest. (Pro tip: Maybe don't use the "smell" metaphor when you ask—that could be awkward and confusing.) Try asking, "If someone asked you what I am passionate about, what would you tell them?" Or ask them, "Do I talk more about being pro-Christ or about being anti-*[fill in the blank]*?"

Do you have non-Christian friends? When it comes to non-Christians, do you do one of the following?

A) Attract them

B) Repel them

C) Neither attract nor repel

D) Condemn them when you talk to your Christian friends

How many of our friends, neighbors, and coworkers would say, like the Ephesians, "We have not even heard there is a Holy Spirit"? They no doubt have heard condemnation from the Christians. Are they hearing the rest of the story about the hope of new and eternal life in Christ from you?

Diagnosis: You stink (it's ok, so do I)

Treatment

Rx: Take a shower, adopt a new scent.

Anyone who has children understands the joys of diaper changes. My one-year-old daughter loves to cry and scream when we change her as if we haven't done this every single day of her life. Not all dirty diapers are created equal, though. Sometimes you can get away with using only a single wipe. Other times . . . oh, those other times. If it's bad enough, you really just have to put on your hazmat suit, strip them down, and get in the shower. When we only had dogs, it was a lot easier to just take them outside and hose them down, but my wife keeps telling me that is not allowed with children. So we make do with the shower.

Based on the Barna studies I cited earlier, many of us Christians are carrying around the shower-worthy stench of hypocrisy, judgment, politics, and condemnation rather than the sweet aroma of the gospel. So how do we wash that off? How do we treat our Gospel Deficiency–induced foul body odor? Fortunately, just like kids have parents to help them, we have the Holy Spirit to help us get cleaned up and smelling nice and fresh again.

First things first, we must ask the Spirit, as David does in Psalm 139:23–24, to help us identify the source of the stench: "Search me, God, and know my heart; test me and know my anxious thoughts. See if there is any offensive way in me and lead me in the way everlasting."

We may not realize what kind of aroma we are emitting. In fact, we are usually the last ones to know that we smell bad, hence the questions in the previous section aimed at getting outside feedback. The Holy Spirit can also reveal to us our true odor and confirm if what others say is true. For example, if we ask the community about their impression of our church and they give answers we don't like, it may be easy to be offended and disregard it. But the Holy Spirit can help confirm (or refute) the validity of those answers. Likewise, if we can't find people to give us brutally honest answers to those diagnostic questions, the Holy Spirit can still point them out to us, if we are willing to listen.

Through this process, as you identify areas of your life that are a bit malodorous, give those over to the Holy Spirit and ask Him to shower you with forgiveness and grace and love as you repent from any sinful source of your sour stench. Some simple examples may be helpful.

Let's say you receive feedback that you or your church are indeed better known for a ministry of condemnation rather than a ministry of reconciliation. Rather than dwell on that and sink into depression and self-despair, let the Lord take that burden from you and give you a new heart for reconciliation. Look for creative ways to repair any breakdown in relationships between you or your church and those around you who may have been hurt by the church. Even if you weren't the ones that hurt them (e.g., they were hurt by another church in the past), this is still a good first step toward reconciliation.

Maybe you or your church are known for "good things" like helping the community, being kind and caring or generous but not for distinctly Christ-like things like evangelism and making new disciples. In this case, the Spirit can lead you to build on the good things you do and begin to pursue even better things that have an eternal impact like explicit gospel proclamation.

These two verses in Psalm 139 also highlight David's anxiety regarding his enemies[5] and his desire for the Lord to lead him into an eternal mindset. These are related. Oftentimes when we have anxious thoughts, they derive from the uncertainty of life and the fears or concerns of living in a fallen world.[6] You may not have people out trying to kill you like David did, but for most Americans today, our anxiety stems from the things of this world: Will I be able to make my next rent payment? Are my children getting a good education? Who is going to win the next election?

Certainly, these aren't inherently bad things to think through and work out, but when we view these things in light of eternity ("the way everlasting") it can quickly reframe our perspective and help our anxiety to dissipate. We will delve deeper into the idea of an eternal mindset in a later chapter.

Those who have fallen into a ministry of condemnation may even do so as a coping mechanism for anxiety. If you watch the news for even five minutes, you will likely see some potentially anxiety-inducing reports that can elicit our fallen nature to respond in unhealthy ways. Let's say, for example, you see on the news that some school districts are starting to teach children things that you don't want your children learning. (This is *completely* hypothetical.) You may automatically start to worry about what your kids' school is teaching (certainly a valid concern). From this, it is an easy jump to turning on the people who may think differently than you, embracing a mindset of condemnation toward "those people." Disagreement on issues is part of life, but it is a fine line to walk between opposing an issue and opposing a person.

It is possible, though not always easy, to engage in civic discourse while at the same time loving the people on the other side of the debate table. Jesus did it. Paul and Peter and the other apostles did it. But it's when we begin to prioritize being right over loving people that things go awry and we lose our distinctly Christ-like aroma.

This is what it all boils down to: prioritizing "love one another" over any other interest or concern we have with one another. Evangelicals prioritizing their politics, being proven right and turning those who disagree with them into the enemy over and above prioritizing love, proving Christ right, and loving our "enemies" is a primary source of losing the aroma of Christ. This directly leads to non-believers labeling us as judgmental hypocrites and identifying us by the things we are against. There were plenty of things Jesus was against, but He never let that get in the way of loving people.

As we saw Paul model to the Ephesians in the book of Acts, we shouldn't be looking to persuade or force people (as if that were possible) into a state of sorrow for their failures, but rather we should invite them into a loving relationship with the Father who runs to meet the prodigals. The Good Shepherd who searches far and wide for the lost sheep. The holy, blameless One who leaves paradise to accept hell on our behalf. Which of these distinctly different ends are we pursuing? Are we spending our time and energy working toward a John baptism or a Jesus baptism?

Going back to 2 Corinthians 2:14 where we started, we are to "spread the aroma of the knowledge of Him everywhere." So what aroma are you spreading? Are people receiving the knowledge of their Savior from you, or are they receiving something lesser than? Even if they are receiving knowledge of something "good" from you, if it is anything less than the gospel of Jesus Christ, there is a serious Gospel Deficiency that needs to be remedied.

Let the Holy Spirit search you and cleanse you from anything that is concealing the aroma of Christ. For some of us, He might have to scrub pretty hard, and it might be painful. You may want to cry and resist like a baby on a changing table, but in the end, we will be fresh and clean and able to fully embrace a new scent of reconciliation that He has for us.

Chapter Three
Pica

Therefore, since we have these promises, dear friends, let us purify ourselves from everything that contaminates body and spirit, perfecting holiness out of reverence for God. (2 Corinthians 7:1)

A young woman presented to the hospital with abdominal pain, constipation, and vomiting. Further evaluation with a CT scan revealed an enlarged, full stomach. A gastroenterologist was consulted to perform an EGD (a test using a light and camera to inspect the stomach and upper digestive tract), which found a large mass composed of whiteish, non-organic material. Upon discussing these findings with the patient, she disclosed that for many years she had been compulsively eating the foam material inside her mattress.[7]

Wait, what? Why? How? This is a typical presentation of a medical disorder known as *pica* (pronunciation rhymes with the name Micah). A simple definition of pica is "the repeated eating of nonfood/nonnutritive substances." This condition can be associated with other various issues like anemia and psychological disorders and may manifest as patients filling up on items like ice chips, corn starch, cotton balls, or any number of nonnutritive items (it's not always mattresses). It may be hard to understand, but it is a very real condition that, although not very common, I have seen on more than one occasion.

People with pica don't just fill up on these nonnutritive items, they actually crave them. Yes, they know about pizza and ice cream and Chick-fil-A and have probably had them all before. And yet, they long to fill their stomachs with nonfood substances.

We might wonder how someone, after experiencing a variety of delicious foods, could possibly crave and long to be filled with these bland, unhealthy, nonnutritive items. Unfortunately, many of us today do the exact same thing when it comes to filling our soul. Despite tasting and seeing that the Lord is good and experiencing His loving presence through the Holy Spirit, we are prone to wander and even gravitate toward filling our spiritual stomachs with garbage that makes us sick.

The Corinthians were apparently drifting into similar territory, which is why Paul admonished them in 6:14–18 (the verses immediately preceding the "therefore" of 7:1 highlighted earlier) to live distinct, holy lives and not fill themselves up with or be contaminated by the things of the world. In their case, these were things like participating in forms of idolatry.

When we see a heading on a passage like this one, which the NIV titles, "Warning Against Idolatry," it is easy to skip past it because we aren't worshipping statues and animals and pagan gods like the people of Bible times. So that section doesn't apply to us, right?

Rather than reducing idolatry to worshipping pagan gods or statues, a better definition for an idol is "anything other than God from which you get your life and worth." Think about that for a second. What gives us life? From where do we derive our self-worth? A good way to test yourself for this is to ask, "If *[fill in the blank]* were taken away from me, would my life feel devoid or meaningless or unsatisfying or unfulfilling? Would I have a bit of an identity crisis if I could no longer identify myself with *[fill in the blank]*?"

Here are some practical examples of things that could be idols based on our working definition:

A sports team

Your career

Political affiliation

Your family

Your theology

Your country

Social media

The list could go on, but hopefully this kickstarts your thinking about what Ezekiel 14:3 calls "idols of the heart" and taking inventory of your own life. In our verse above, Paul said, "Let us purify ourselves from everything that contaminates body and spirit." The phrase "everything that contaminates body and spirit" likely brings to mind illicit drugs, drunkenness, and pornography. Or sex, drugs, and rock & roll, as they would say in past generations. Certainly, these things can and do contaminate both body and spirit (he says while simultaneously listening to rock & roll), but these external vices are often emphasized to the exclusion of others. Because of this, we are particularly vulnerable to these sneakier, internal, idols of the heart.

When looking at that list of possible idols (and again, you may have your own), it may be hard to think about something like family as contaminating body and spirit. Timothy Keller says, "We think that idols are bad things, but that is almost never the case. The greater the good, the more likely we are to expect that it can satisfy our deepest needs and hopes. Anything can serve as a counterfeit god, especially the very best things in life."[8] In this case, the contamination may not come from the thing itself but from the place it holds in our heart. Any good thing can be elevated in our lives to the point that we actually place it on a throne and derive our sense of self-worth and identity from it. In other words, we worship it.

Whatever idols exist in our life, they likely started from us filling up on non–spiritually nutritive things. Maybe seeking the praise of others in the workplace or high achievements started you on the path to the idolatry of career, which has become your source of self-worth. Maybe consuming too much cable news grew your identification with a political party to the point that you can no longer separate the two because your political party *is* your identity, or at least a big part of it. You can think through the origins of any idols in your own life, but it all comes back to filling up on things other than God.

The things that give us our sense of self and identity and fulfillment apart from Christ and His Word are no different than eating a mattress or cotton balls. We are filling up on soul food that is nonnutritive and unhealthy.

Like the old saying goes, you are what you eat. Insofar as we are filled with the Spirit and abiding in Christ, we will reflect His love and glory to the world around us. Conversely, to the extent that we fill up on the things of the world, we *become* like the world. Finding our worth and value and fulfillment from the world rather than being filled with the Spirit is a strong indicator of Gospel Deficiency.

Reflectors

To be fair, just because you consume social media or have a favorite sports team, that doesn't necessarily mean it has risen to the level of idolatry. It is possible to engage with these things while also receiving all your life and worth and identity from Christ. We are, however, prone to reflect the things that consume our time and energy and presence. Just like Moses coming down from the mountain radiating the glory of God after being in His presence (2 Corinthians 3:7–18), what we fill our lives with will be reflected to those around us.

Do we reflect the Lord's glory? Or do we reflect the computer screen or phone we stare at all day? Do we regurgitate the news and views we are fed through media, or does the love of Christ overflow within us like a wellspring of water ready to satiate the dry, cracked lips of a thirsty and dying world? Moses reflected the Lord's glory after spending time with Him. He couldn't help it. He didn't choose it. It was a natural byproduct of being in the Lord's presence.

The converse example is Gollum from *Lord of the Rings*, who reflected the evil in the ring of power. It seemed like a nice, harmless ring at first, but the longer he stayed with it, the more it corrupted him until he was unrecognizable from his former self. Politics and money and a whole host of worldly things can have the same effect on us. It starts out seemingly innocent or well intentioned, but over time it can turn us into a completely different person. I experienced my own Gollum-ing firsthand.

There was a time in my life when I was heavily invested in politics. I followed a constant stream of news updates on my phone, kept up with all the latest scandals, interviewed to work on a political campaign, and even wrote for a political website.

But it didn't take long for me to notice my heart changing. My days were dictated by who was leading in the polls or who said what salacious thing the day before. I began disparaging people I disagreed with and looking at life through the lens of red and blue. The prospect and pursuit of political power was taking its toll as if it were the ring power. It was when I realized this that I decided I had to retire from politics physically, mentally, and emotionally. I had to get out. It was corrosive and corrupting. I had become a political Gollum. Thankfully, the Lord saved me from that.

Whether we spend our time with the Lord or consuming politics or media or anything else, we are going to reflect that. Our mind is malleable and morphs into what it consumes. And what we consume will end up consuming us. The mouth speaks from the overflow of the heart (Matthew 12:34). For example, if you watch sports all day, you're going to talk about the sports. If you consume celebrity gossip or wellness blogs all the time, what comes out of your life and mouth is going to reflect that. What would it look like to be so consumed with the presence of the Spirit that we can't help but reflect His glory and speak about Him to others?

Diagnostics: Nutrition Inventory

What are you filling up on day-by-day? What sustains you? Is it the Spirit and the Word of God, or something else?

I described the corruptive effects politics had on me. Is there anything in your life, past or present, that has a similar effect on you? Is it time for you to establish a healthy distance from it or even retire like I did?

You are what you eat. If you are filled up with the Spirit, your life will necessarily bear the fruit of the Spirit (Galatians 5:22–23). We can't really measure our "filledness" with the Spirit, but we can take inventory of the fruit that comes when the Spirit is in us. Are these present in your life in all circumstances and with all people?

Love (even for your enemies?)

Joy (even in the midst of hardship?)

Peace (even in times of conflict?)

Patience (even when you're on a tight schedule?)

Kindness (even when you're in a hurry?)

Goodness (even when you're treated badly?)

Faithfulness (even when you're busy?)

Gentleness (even when you're angry?)

Self-control (even when you're being attacked?)

In 1 Corinthians 3:3–4, Paul said, "You are still worldly. For since there is jealousy and quarreling among you, are you not worldly? Are you not acting like mere humans? For when one says, 'I follow Paul,' and another, 'I follow Apollos,' are you not mere human beings?" Do you participate in quarreling, particularly with other Christians? Do you argue about which human you follow rather than following Christ alone?

A. W. Tozer once said, "If the Holy Spirit was withdrawn from the church today, 95 percent of what we do would go on and no one would know the difference." Is this true of your church? If not 95 percent, what percentage would go on unchanged without the Holy Spirit?

Chapter Three

Diagnosis: Junk food adddict

Treatment

Rx: Detox/cleanse followed by diet modifications

God is pretty good at making stuff. He designed our bodies to self-regulate and get rid of things that can cause us harm through organs like the kidneys, liver, and GI tract. Because God is a good Creator, there really isn't a physical or medical need for people to do cleanses or detoxes for their body despite the many diet fads and products you may see advertised. Our mind and souls, on the other hand, are a different story.

We have seen how all kinds of toxic things (or good things causing toxic effects) can infiltrate our thinking and make us quite unhealthy spiritually. These sorts of toxins can build up over time and can be hard to purge. In this case, a spiritual cleanse or detox can actually be beneficial. It may not be easy and you may feel the pains of withdrawal, but you will be spiritually healthier because of it.

The first thing to do is to identify any toxic thing that you are regularly consuming and stop it. This may be social media, news, video games, anything that is filling a void in your life that should only be filled by the Holy Spirit. As with a lot of addictions, cold turkey is very effective, but you may have better success by tapering off gradually. Either way, the first step is to stop consuming new toxins.

The next step is to go on a spiritual cleanse. Just as some people do a juice cleanse where they only consume juice for a period of time, we can benefit from a spiritual cleanse where we fast from certain things that occupy our life and instead only consume the

Word of God, letting the Holy Spirit fill our soul. As we are increasingly filled with the gospel truth, the gospel will naturally begin to overflow out of our lives to those around us.

First Corinthians 2:12 tells us, "What we have received is not the spirit of the world, but the Spirit who is from God, so that we may understand what God has freely given us." The Spirit that we have is from God, not from the world. Sometimes, though, the things of the world can accumulate in our system so much that it hinders us from hearing and being led by the Spirit. Just like an accumulated blockage in the coronary arteries hinders blood flow in a heart attack, impeding the Holy Spirit in our life can cause irreparable damage. We are God's temple (1 Corinthians 3:16) where His Spirit resides, so it behooves us and honors Him to keep His temple tidy.

Once we have successfully completed our cleanse, the final step is to keep all that junk from coming back in. Job 34:3 says, "The ear tests words like the tongue tastes food."[9] We must train our ears to be as discerning as our tongue and spit out anything rotten our ears taste. Over time we will learn to quickly and easily identify gospel-deficient talk so that we can reject it before it has a chance to poison us. Whether it be things that we are prone to idolize or just plain bad things that do not honor Christ, the quicker we "spit them out" of our ears and eyes, the healthier our system will remain and the more clearly we can hear His voice.

Like the old worship song "Give Us Clean Hands" says, "Let us not lift our soul to another."[10] We are not our own. We were bought at a price. And not a cheap one. We were bought with the precious blood of Christ. So when we lift our souls to another, we are stealing what is rightfully God's.

In Mark 12:17, Jesus says, "Give back to Caesar what is Caesar's and to God what is God's." In this specific story the discussion is about money, but what if this command applies to more than just money? What if it applies to everything we have—our time, our effort, our very lives? If everything we have, including our lives, belongs to God because He purchased us, once we give Him what is rightfully His, there is nothing left for Caesar or any other false idol.

When Jesus first called his disciples to follow Him, they left behind their fishing gear, which was their livelihood (Matthew 4:18–22). There is nothing inherently bad or sinful about fishing. It is a good thing that feeds people and provides for the fisherman's family. But they left it behind for something better. They left it to follow Jesus with their whole heart.

The question for us now is not if we should follow Jesus. The question for us is, What do we need to leave behind so that we can follow Him with our whole heart? If Jesus calls us to leave behind good things to follow Him, how much more do we need to cleanse ourselves from the toxic things of the world that contaminate our body and soul?

Chapter Four
Myopia

"So we fix our eyes not on what is seen, but on what is unseen, since what is seen is temporary, but what is unseen is eternal."
(2 Corinthians 4:18)

The African country in which I live was recently ranked as the poorest, least developed country in the world. This is based on metrics like economy, access to health care, education, and infrastructure. On the flip side, I was born and raised in the wealthiest country in the world. It was a drastic transition that, in many ways, I am still adjusting to years later. Compassionate people back in the United States often ask us how they can help, inquiring, "What is the biggest need you see there?"

As a doctor, I see some of the most extreme cases of treatable diseases. Despite the availability of a cure, many people do not have access to health care or the means to afford it, so they don't seek medical help until it's almost too late. Unfortunately, all too often, it *is* too late. We also see massive amounts of malnutrition in children due to lack of access to affordable food. The list of needs could go on, but suffice it to say, the physical and social needs are as significant as you will find anywhere in the world.

Amid all of these struggles, how do I answer questions about the biggest need? Easy. The biggest need here is the gospel. And it's not even close. This country is less than 1 percent Christian, leaving millions and millions of people living and dying without the gospel. As great as the financial and development disparity is between my passport country and my country of residence, the greatest disparity and injustice between the two is access to the gospel. Opportunity to hear and respond to the gospel is the greatest need of every person in every country on earth. Most Christians would agree with this, but is that reflected in our day-to-day life?

Short-Sighted or Eternally Minded

In this section of Paul's second letter to the Corinthians, he was explaining to them all the trouble and hardship he had faced for the sake of the gospel. In 4:8–12 Paul said that he was hard-pressed on every side (v. 8), persecuted (v. 9), and struck down (v. 9). As if that were not enough, in verses 10–12 he said that he was always carrying around the death of Jesus in his body (v. 10), he was constantly being given over to death (v. 11), and death was at work in him (v. 12). Death, death, and more death.

That all sounds pretty bleak, but when you read about all the beatings and murderous attempts on his life, you have to know he not only felt like death but probably also looked like it. The amazing thing is that despite all of that, he went on to say in verse 14–17, "We know that the one who raised the Lord Jesus from the dead will also raise us with Jesus. . . . Therefore we do not lose heart. Though outwardly we are wasting away, yet inwardly we are being renewed day by day. For our light and momentary troubles are achieving for us an eternal glory that far outweighs them all."

This leads right into 4:18, highlighted at the beginning of this chapter, which emphasizes the need to keep our eyes fixed on the eternal rather than the temporary. In the midst of all the trouble and heartache and beatings, Paul learned to keep his eyes fixed on the glory of God and the future of His kingdom coming in fullness to right all the wrongs. He did not look at his hardships or even his attackers in human terms. No, he saw all of this through the lens of eternity. He kept his eyes fixed on what is everlasting: the love of God, the salvation received through the blood of Christ, the constant presence of the Holy Spirit, and his mission to proclaim the good news around the world. All of these other things will pass away. As the old hymn "Turn Your Eyes Upon Jesus" puts it, if you keep your eyes fixed on Him, "The things of earth will grow strangely dim, in the light of His glory and grace."[11]

A gospel-deficient life will always gravitate toward a view of life through the lens of the here and now. When hardship and trouble befall us, we may fall into anxiety or despair or anger. *How could this happen? This will ruin everything!* It seems like every week, or even every day, there is a new outrage about some event that happened. You can spend about thirty seconds on social media and find ten new things the world is mad about today. Maybe some dirt was exposed about a politician. Perhaps the market is in a slump. Maybe a celebrity did something scandalous. Shocking!

These are all relatively trivial occurrences, but sometimes the outrage pertains to bigger issues like racial injustice, global pandemics, or unequal access to health care around the world. These, and others, are certainly issues worth discussing and looking for solutions. Once again, this book is not trying to address these issues specifically or to advocate for complete withdrawal from the world. The bigger issue is about priority and emphasis. The point here is to demonstrate how easily these temporal, worldly troubles and the scandals *du jour* keep our eyes fixed on the here and now to the neglect of the eternal kingdom where our true citizenship resides.

This nearsightedness not only applies to our view of circumstances, but also to the people around us. We often view others through the lens of the world. We see them with earthly labels (e.g., coworker, neighbor, Republican, Democrat, rich, poor) or categorize them in worldly terms as good or bad depending on how they affect us and our interests. *My barista is the best; she gives me extra whipped cream. My neighbor is the worst; he plays his music too loud.* It's probably not as extreme as Paul's enemies trying to kill him, but nevertheless, this way of thinking is still there inside us.

In terms of seeing others through the lens of eternity, Paul wrote in 5:16 that in light of eternity, in light of what Christ has done for us (v. 14), and in light of Christ dying for all and thereby ascribing unsurpassable worth to them (v. 15), "we regard no one from a worldly point of view."

What does it mean to regard others from a worldly point of view? And when (not "if") we do, how do we change that? You can think of examples from your own life, but to get to the point, any way of viewing people—other than as beloved sons and daughters of our Father in heaven who sent His Son to die for them and whose Spirit is pursuing them to lead them to salvation and to whom we are called to proclaim the gospel—is probably a worldly point of view. How often do we view people this way?

An optimistic view of these type of responses to circumstances and people is that our focus on the temporary is just misplaced groaning for heaven. Just after this passage, in 5:2 Paul stated, "Meanwhile we groan, longing to be clothed instead with our heavenly dwelling." All of us have a sense that the world is not how it is supposed to be, and we have a hope for a bright, eternal future with the Lord. Verse 5:5 explains that all Christians have been "given the Spirit as a deposit, guaranteeing what is to come." The Holy Spirit inside of us gives us a glimpse of eternity, and in fact, He works in us so that we might be a signpost pointing others to eternal life.

The breakdown comes when we become increasingly nearsighted (myopic) and the things of earth become big and we lose sight of eternity. In contrast to the hymn, we turn our eyes on the world and look full in all the wonders and concerns of the here and now. And the things of heaven grow strangely dim in the light of our glory and well-being. We become fixated on things like health and wealth, power and success. We view others as with us or against us. Our selfish default is to view people through the lens of our temporary needs rather than their eternal needs. We focus on feeding our bodies here and now rather than feeding our souls toward eternity. That's Gospel Deficiency.

Blind Spots

Beyond circumstances and people, there are also *issues*. When discussing the idea of an eternal mindset, American churches have tended to emphasize points such as, "You can't take your money to heaven," and, "Don't work for success or to please other people; work for the Lord." Whether we let those lessons take root in our heart is another story, but at least this good teaching is there. Unfortunately, our Christian culture tends to have many Gospel Deficiency–induced blind spots. And it's not just that we miss them; we often actually justify them in Christian lingo and wrap them up as a godly cause to promote the ways of this world. These are things that, though not inherently sinful, keep our eyes strongly fixed on the world to the neglect of the eternal. Here are a few examples, but many more could be given.

Health. Since I was a kid, I have seen America go through drastic changes in terms of how we view health. When I was young, no one really asked how many calories were in something or what type of fat is in this or that. Increasing consciousness about what we put in our bodies is a great thing, and it certainly makes my job as a physician much easier. But now some people have gone to the other extreme, where they live as if fitness is next to godliness. They cling to their earthly bodies like it could be better than the one they will get in heaven. Again, healthy eating and exercise are great things, but it can easily become an obsession and one more thing that pulls your eyes off eternity. (See also 1 Timothy 4:7–10; 1 Corinthians 15:50–54.)

Family. As good and great as family is, it is a distinctly worldly way to categorize people. That doesn't mean we love them or care for them any less or neglect them. But it is possible for our nuclear family to become the nucleus of our entire life to the neglect of everything else outside of it, including Christ himself. Rather than pursuing the eternal good of others, maybe we fixate on the temporal good of our kids. Don't get me wrong—you definitely should keep taking care of your kids. But temporal, familial well-being in this world should not overshadow the eternal well-being of others.

Politics. There is nothing in life that people are more passionate about that is more temporal and short-sighted than politics. It's so short-sighted that there are twenty-four-hour news channels that bounce from topic to topic with short news cycles and shorter memories about whatever bombshell or scandal happened just a few days before. Everything is catastrophic until the next catastrophe happens, and we move on to that one. On top of that, politics has nothing to do with eternity, and it sure can't lead people to Christ. Even if we have good intentions getting involved in politics, we can extrapolate from the aforementioned Barna studies that Christians' involvement in politics has done far more to turn people off from Christ than point them to him. It is only in receiving and living the gospel that political, economic, and other questions can be solved and by which people can be freed from the bonds of sin and death.

This is obviously not an exhaustive list of blind spots that impair our vision. Certainly, you can think of others in your life and church and community. These are just the low-hanging fruit that have become ubiquitous in American Christian culture.

Whether we are talking about circumstances or people or issues, everything we see and do should be in light of eternity and the gospel of Christ. Even if you are in the poorest country in the world facing a constant stream of patients who are sick and dying, we cannot lose sight of the world's biggest need. An eternal, gospel-focused mindset should color and influence and filter every aspect of our lives. To the extent that it does not, we are withholding these areas of our life from the Spirit's influence.

Diagnostics: Vision Check

What do you set your eyes on more often: the temporary or the eternal? For an objective assessment, look at your bank statement and screen time on your phone. Think back to the conversations you've had over the last week. Are you investing your money, time, and energy in the temporary or the eternal?

Do you define problems the way the world does, or do you see through the eyes of Christ? Apart from the Spirit we are unable to see the spiritual reality in which we are struggling. We see only the surface of social, political, and economic problems, and therefore we only work on the surface. Our job is to let the Spirit show us a new way of seeing and to discover the real spiritual difficulty that every social, political, and economic situation contains. Will you let the Spirit reframe your vision to see with new eyes?

Are your thoughts and life and heart controlled by the world, or do they belong to the Lord? Christians have a distinct calling and purpose that no one else can fulfill. If we act the same way as everyone else or support institutions and purposes of the world, we are no different. Are you different?

What are we trying to convert people to? What are our actions and words pointing toward? Health? Moralism? Cultural values? Is it anything that would lead people to Christ? The road to salvation is not paved with health, wealth, moralism, or the American way but with the blood of Jesus Christ. He alone has the power to save. Do you spend your time trying to persuade people toward Christ or toward something else? Do you spend more time thinking of "the others" (i.e., those who think and act and believe differently than you) as those in need of repentance from their opinions rather than as spiritual captives in need of eternal rescue? Picture someone on the other side of the political aisle. Where does your mind go? Do you automatically feel defensive or aggressive? Or do you feel the love of the Father who ascribed to that person unsurpassable worth by dying for them on the cross?

Diagnosis: Vision impairment

Treatment
Rx: Gospel Glasses

Have you ever read stories or watched videos online about color-blind people seeing color for the first time? It is truly touching and fun to watch. These peoples' literal view of the world completely changes and they finally see creation in all its colorful glory. This is made possible by special-made glasses that provide an external correction for the internal cause of the colorblindness.

In order to correct our nearsightedness, we need corrective lenses. That is what I am calling our Gospel Glasses. These glasses enable us to see the outside world and the people around us through the lens of the gospel and give us an eternal perspective. Just as 1 Corinthians 2:16 talks about us having "the mind of Christ," this is akin to having the eyes of Christ, to see each day and each other through the loving, compassionate eyes of the Savior who determined that this world and all its inhabitants are worth dying for. We can gain the eyes of Christ by following the will of the Spirit.

Returning to the speeches in Acts, when the Holy Spirit comes at Pentecost, we see Peter and the apostles inspired and driven to confront the very people who murdered their friend and Savior. Talk about difficult circumstances and people! Not long before this, Peter was slicing off ears to defend Jesus. But now, empowered and inspired by the Holy Spirit, Peter did not confront them with hostility or anger or even attempt to prove Christ's innocence. Rather, he confronted them with the good news so that they too may be saved. Apart from the Holy Spirit, Peter cut to the body with a sword to draw blood. With the Holy Spirit he "cut to the heart" (Acts 2:37), preaching the saving grace of the blood of Christ.

This is the approach we should have toward others, even our enemies. Our primary focus should not be to change their behavior or chastise them for their misdeeds. Our overwhelming focus should be on their salvation and acceptance of Christ as Lord of their life. Too often we meet opposition with force. This is an all-too-human response to seek to gain power over opposition to right their wrongs. But the model we see here is that when the Holy Spirit is leading the way, we meet opposition with love and the spiritual force of the gospel. This force alone, the gospel that is the power of God, the same power that raised Christ from the dead, proclaimed in the power of the Holy Spirit, is the force by which we should confront opposition and enemies.

We should not seek primarily to argue and debate, though there may be occasion when this is appropriate. But too often this is our primary response above and before the gospel. Keep in mind that winning a debate or constructing a better argument is not the power of God for salvation. That mantle belongs to the gospel alone. When we come face-to-face with opposition or enemies, whether it be political or social or personal, we should release our white-knuckle grip on the reigns of self-justification and submit to the working of the Holy Spirit, who seeks salvation of "the other" more than anything else. If salvation is the primary focus of the Spirit, it should be ours as well.

This is difficult to do in our own power since arguments and opposition elicit our fight-or-flight response, which inherently makes us less rational. Therefore, our "natural" instincts or reasoning in these situations are often not trustworthy. Let's let the Spirit do the thinking and reacting for us and speak to the only thing that eternally matters: the person standing in front of us or online is a beloved human for whom Christ died and who is in need of a Savior. Their eternal destiny is more important than any human disagreement, even a disagreement as big as the unjust murder of the innocent King of the Universe. If the Spirit can see past that to focus on the good news and salvation of "the other," surely He can help us look past things like political differences or other disagreements that have no bearing on eternity.

Jesus said to love your neighbor, and Peter, in Acts 2:40 admonished his hearers to save themselves from the corruption of the world. Unfortunately, rather than love our neighbor and save ourselves from the things of the world, all too often we are found loving this world and trying to save ourselves from our neighbors. We engage in the things of this world and fight the way the world does. Ephesians 6:12 reminds us that our battle is not against flesh and blood, but the increasingly polarized culture of America today has even turned Christians on each other (more on this later). Rather than being known by our love for each other (John 13:35), Christians are increasingly known by their love for themselves, their agendas, and their politics.

Wanting to influence society for the better is not inherently evil, but some Christians become so desirous to transform society and culture that they tend to forget that real, heart-level cultural transformation comes about as a result of lives transformed by the eternal gospel. By focusing on transforming society and neglecting the gospel, the eternal tends to be eclipsed by the temporal.[12]

When the world is our priority, we invest more and more in things that matter less and less until we end up giving up everything for nothing. In Matthew 16:26, Jesus asked, "What good will it be for someone to gain the whole world, yet forfeit their soul?" Likewise, I would ask, if we gain the whole world, convince everyone to adopt our opinions and way of living and vote the way we do, but we lose their souls, what good have we done?

We have an opportunity and privilege to bear witness to another way of life, an eternal life. We can be a signpost pointing people to the kingdom of God and inviting them into communion with their loving Savior. But if we spend our life focused on things that will all pass away, it is an opportunity and a responsibility squandered. And it is those who never hear the gospel who pay the price. For eternity.

An eternal perspective, seeing the world through Gospel Glasses, shows us that we can either invest our lives in our temporary, or others', eternity: "The church should embrace 'final destiny' as the chief constraining factor in all of its interactions with the world."[13] What would it look like for you and your church to embrace "final destiny," or eternal destiny, as the guiding factor in all your interactions with the people around you? Would that change how you see and relate to them? Looking through this lens and pointing them to Jesus through sharing the gospel may be a challenge for your temporary life, but it could be their start on a path to eternal life.

Don't let the world set your agenda for the day. Don't let the talking heads on TV or the comments on social media steer your mind away from eternity. Our Lord has given us our agenda: to love our neighbors and make disciples. In this we no longer view others from the point of view of the world but through the eyes of Christ. Looking through the eyes of Christ and growing in the love of Christ for others will enable us to deliberately substitute God's perfect interests in other people for our selfish interests in them.

Prayer for Vision Correction

Adjusting your eyes to see through Gospel Glasses begins and ends with prayer. We must pray daily that the Lord would give us eyes to see as He does. We must pray to see the world and others as He does. This vision correction can only come from Him working in us. He is the Great Ophthalmologist, the Great Heart Surgeon, and He alone can perform this miraculous work in us.

Prayer must also be our immediate response to hardship and our enemies. Give those concerns to the Lord, and let Him show you how to view that situation or person. When you see someone as problematic or evil or any other worldly label, turn that perception to prayer. Maybe you even discern correctly that that person has some issues. But as Oswald Chambers says, "Discernment is God's call to intercession, never to fault finding."[14]

During these prayers for others, particularly for those we find difficult to love, it can help to imagine that person while asking God to show you how to view them. Imagine Jesus walking up to them and how He would interact with them. Oftentimes when I do this, God brings to mind the story of the woman caught in adultery in John 8. Except this time, it is me holding the stones. And when Jesus bends down to write in the sand, He writes my sins, one after another, until I drop my stone and walk away as the Pharisees did.

An eternal perspective means viewing your life and others in light of eternity. Looking at life through the lens of the cross means letting the gospel define our perspective on everything we see, think, and do. This combination of an eternal perspective through the lens of the cross are your Gospel Glasses. If we wake up and put on our Gospel Glasses every day, it will radically change everything we do and could radically change everyone around us.

Chapter Five
Impotence

"If our gospel is veiled, it is veiled to those who are perishing. The god of this age has blinded the minds of unbelievers, so that they cannot see the light of the gospel that displays the glory of Christ, who is the image of God. For what we preach is not ourselves, but Jesus Christ as Lord, and ourselves as your servants for Jesus' sake. For God, who said, "Let light shine out of darkness," made his light shine in our hearts to give us the light of the knowledge of God's glory displayed in the face of Christ. But we have this treasure in jars of clay to show that this all-surpassing power is from God and not from us." (2 Corinthians 4:3–7)

I walked into my college classroom one day and all the lights were off. I asked the two students who arrived before me why the lights were off and they told me the lights weren't working. It seemed odd since other lights in the building were on, but maybe this room just had some isolated electrical issue. It was an old building, so who knows? I took their word for it and joined them in the dark. As more students walked in, those of us sitting in the dark passed on the news about the broken lights. Eventually, the professor walked into a classroom full of students sitting in the dark. Rather than asking why the lights were off, as the students did, she just flipped the light switch. And guess what happened? The lights miraculously came on! She had fixed the electrical issue. Except the real electrical issue was not in the building but in the brain of the students who were told there was no power and simply took others' word for it.

Let There Be Light

As Paul continues his second letter to the Corinthians, the latter half of chapter 3 and on through chapter 4 addresses the reality that there is a battle for the minds and souls of all people. The theme of a veil set between the truth and glory of God and the mind of unbelievers references Moses coming down from the mountain and having to wear a veil over his face. This was because he had caught a glimpse of the glory of God. He came down glowing, and the grumbling Israelites could not stand to look at it.

In this case, Moses, as the reflector of the glory of God, covered himself for the sake of others. Similarly, in the Jewish temple, there was a curtain set up to veil the holy of holies since, you know, people could drop dead from experiencing it. However, when Jesus was crucified that temple curtain was torn from top to bottom, signifying the end of that separation. God's presence would no longer reside in the temple but within His people.

This ties into 2 Corinthians 4, where we see that, in a bit of a reversal, it was the unbelievers who were veiled (v. 4, "blinded the minds of unbelievers") rather than God's presence or glory being veiled. And in this case, it was Satan doing the veiling in a malicious way rather than God (or Moses, in his case) veiling in a helpful way.

In this passage, Paul elucidates the spiritual war that is going on between light and darkness. It is a battle for the souls and salvation of all humankind. And the way this battle is won is through proclamation of the powerful gospel of Jesus Christ to set the captives free so that they may run into the marvelous light of their loving Creator. Let's break it down.

First, in verse 4 we see what Satan is up to in this war: he is blinding the minds of unbelievers so they cannot see the truth of the gospel. Those who are far from God, from the atheist to the jihadist, likely are not in their respective camp because they want to be far from God on their own accord. Paul says those who don't believe in Christ, no matter the reason, are being blinded by Satan. Therefore, we should view unbelievers not as wrong people to be opposed or defeated, but as captives who need to be liberated from the subjugation of a wicked tyrant.

At the same time, verse 6 shows us what God is up to: He is shining His light and glory, which are most clearly revealed in the face of Christ. On top of that, He has made this light shine within His people so that all may know Him and see Him more clearly. Just as He spoke light out of darkness, so also the Holy Spirit illuminates our darkened hearts and minds to see the truth to which Satan is trying to blind us.

With Satan acting on one side and God on the other, where do we fit in? Verse 5 shows us our role right in the middle of the cosmic battle: we preach Jesus Christ as Lord. Spirit-filled people proclaiming the gospel of Christ is God's means of transferring people from Satan's kingdom to that of His kingdom (Acts 26:18). We proclaim the gospel boldly as the power of God to set the captives free and to lift the Satan-imposed veil from their eyes. We show the world what it means to be servants of the Most High God. We do not proclaim ourselves as the saviors of the world or the ones with all the answers. We are but feeble, fragile jars of clay. As Paul said, we resolve to know and trust only in Christ and Him crucified (1 Corinthians 2:2). Nothing else will do.

Chapter Five

Perceived Impotence

Herein lies the backdrop for the fourth symptom of Gospel Deficiency: impotence. Or, more accurately, *perceived* impotence—perceived impotence of the gospel—which, for all intents and purposes, leads to practical impotence of God's people. A weakened view of the gospel manifests as a weakened, nonreproducing ministry of the church. None of us would actually say that we have a weakened view of the gospel, and you may be thinking that even now. *Not me!* But once again, our actions reveal the truth.

Let's first look at how Paul trusted in the power of the gospel for salvation for all people. Just a few verses before the passage with which we started this chapter, in 4:2 Paul states that he relied on "setting forth the truth plainly" rather than relying on the worldly ways of persuading people. Even before that in 3:14, Paul states that "only in Christ is [the veil] taken away." Relying on the gospel as the power of God to do the heavy lifting was not unique to Corinth. All throughout the book of Acts, we see Paul (as well as all the other apostles and disciple-makers) engaging people with the gospel alone and trusting that the gospel is sufficient to change lives. It was the power of the gospel and the working of the Holy Spirit in those who heard the good news that completely upended the cultures and cities and regions in which it took hold.

But what about us? If we want to see people come to Christ, do we rely on the gospel alone? When we talk about "outreach" or "missions" do we simply preach the good news and trust that is enough? Or do we turn to things like programs and events and gimmicks? Do we think social projects like serving the homeless or building a house carries more weight than the gospel itself or is somehow necessary to give the gospel more power and credibility?

If we want to change lives, cultures, cities, and regions, how do we go about it? What do we rely on and put our hope in to do the heavy lifting? For those who want to "save America" or "make it great," what are the means you are pursuing toward that end? Is it through the gospel, "setting forth the truth plainly," as Paul did? Do you work to change lives and minds by preaching Christ and Him crucified in whom alone the veil can be lifted? Or are you preaching the power of something lesser?

Our modern Christian culture in America has increasingly relied on things like power, politics, and programs to make impactful change in our society. And this is not unique to any one particular political party or group. Across the board, many Christians in America turn to the things of this world to change the things of this world rather than turning to eternal things to make eternal change. As David Garland notes in his commentary on 2 Corinthians, "Humans make themselves susceptible to [Satan's] wiles with their preoccupation with the transient, unspiritual, earthly realm."[15]

To be clear, pursuing societal change and affecting lives is a good thing to do. The issue here is the means by which we go about it. We may start with good intentions, but we turn to the things of the world because we, knowingly or unknowingly, don't believe the gospel is enough to achieve our intended good.

Want to end poverty? Or abortion? Or corruption? OK, then, whose power do you turn to for this? Have you ever considered that the power of the gospel could achieve all of this? If not or if you don't believe it's possible, maybe it's because you have a weak view of the gospel. Have you tried a gospel-first approach and found that it failed, or have you failed to even try? Maybe you are sitting in a dark room because of a mistaken belief that the power is out when you haven't even tried the light switch.

The gospel is the only means that our King has given us by which to see His kingdom come on earth as in heaven. Not earthly power. Not politics. Not money or our clever programs. Our focus should be on peoples' hearts, which will lead to societal change; societal change cannot change hearts. This is politics through living rather than politics through voting. Looking to other means over and above the gospel to change lives is a clear sign of Gospel Deficiency in ours.

Diagnostics

How do you and your church do outreach and missions? In those ministries, how prominent is evangelism? Are these ministries characterized more by works like service projects or by the explicit sharing of the gospel? If you took evangelism out of these ministries, how different would they look?

How do you primarily pursue social change in your area? Is it by engaging people with the gospel or by some other means? Do you believe the gospel has more or less power to affect social change than those "other means" (e.g., politics, social programs, money)?

In the last four years, which of these activities have you done more: (1) Vote or (2) share the full gospel with a nonbeliever in an attempt to lead them to Christ?

When you or your church or ministry seek to influence the outside world and change your community for the better, is Christ necessary to accomplish your mission? Is there something about this work that can only be done through the power of Christ that

Impotence

wealthy, non-Christian humanitarians or social or political activists couldn't also do? What are you doing for which Christ is necessary? What are you relying on God for that a wealthy lobbyist could not also achieve? What end are you pursuing that also could be achieved by those without the Holy Spirit? Is the world you are trying to build a world built on the blood of Christ? If a non-Christian could build the same world, the answer is an emphatic *no*. When we see the grand story of the Bible and all that transpired, we see that God's hand was necessary through it all. We do see, from time to time, God working through nonbelievers in a sense (e.g., hardening Pharaoh's heart, Paul talking about nonbelievers sharing the gospel), but what He eternally accomplished through His people could not be done by nonbelievers. The changing of hearts toward Him cannot be done apart from the power of the Holy Spirit in the gospel, which is the power of God for salvation. Atheist humanitarians can (and do) build wonderful hospitals in Africa, advocate for legislation that you might agree with, and feed the hungry. So what are we doing that they can't? What are we doing for which Christ is necessary?[16]

Diagnosis: Misunderstanding the Gospel

Treatment

Rx: Education about the power of the gospel; repeat as needed

Where we live in Africa, the vast majority of people are dependent on farming to provide food for their family. Everyone farms and knows about farming. Each year when the rainy season approaches, our African friends like to jokingly ask me about my farm. They know I don't have a farm, and they know I don't know

59

anything about farming, which they find hilarious and preposterous.

One year I actually wanted to try to grow a few things, so I sought out a friend for advice. I had a ton of questions about what to do and how to do it. At one point, after a list of questions, he simply said, "You just put the seed in the ground and wait. It will take care of the rest." As an experienced seed sower, my friend knew that the power of growth resides in the seed, not the sower, just as we see in the parable of the growing seed in Mark 4:26–29.

The Powerful Seed

How do we treat our Gospel Deficiency–induced impotence? When it comes to making disciples or positively influencing society or making the world a better place, we must recognize that the gospel is the most powerful tool to make this happen. If the gospel is not able to bring about the change we seek in the world, perhaps we are seeking the wrong type of change. The gospel is the tool our Lord has given us with which to engage the world. In order to recognize that, we must begin to recognize the gospel as the power of God.

Romans 1:16 tells us that "the gospel . . . is the power of God that brings salvation to everyone who believes." To understand this, we need to have a good grasp on both "the gospel" and "the power of God." We attempted to define "the gospel" in an earlier chapter, so the next task is to understand "the power of God."

The Power of God

From speaking all creation into existence, to making a covenant with Abraham and giving him a son when "his body was as good as dead . . . Sarah's womb was also dead" (Romans 4:19) and then

God himself fulfilling that covenant in Jesus, the entire Bible is essentially one long narrative displaying God's power.

We see the power of the presence of God in the Old Testament narrative of the Israelites. God led them out of Egypt and then across parted waters (twice!) and fed them from the sky. Oh, and don't forget about the ark of the covenant, the tabernacle, and the temple where God's powerful presence resided. During this time, there were people who would drop dead just from being too close to God's power in an unworthy manner. Battles were won, enemies were defeated, and the earth stopped spinning as the sun stood still in the sky all in the name and power of the Lord.

The biblical narrative climaxes in the person of Jesus Christ, who is the ultimate display of the power of God. As if a virgin birth weren't impressive enough, Jesus goes on to heal the sick, open the eyes of the blind, raise the dead, calm the storms, and exert His authority over Satan and demons. And soon thereafter we see the ultimate expression of His power in His death and resurrection:

> [Jesus,] who, being in very nature God, did not consider equality with God something to be used to his own advantage; rather, he made himself nothing by taking the very nature of a servant, being made in human likeness. And being found in appearance as a man, he humbled himself by becoming obedient to death—even death on a cross! Therefore God exalted him to the highest place and gave him the name that is above every name, that at the name of Jesus every knee should bow, in heaven and on earth and under the earth, and every tongue acknowledge that Jesus Christ is Lord, to the glory of God the Father. (Philippians 2:6–11)

This is what we are talking about when we say, "the power of God." Yet for some of us, God's power has become an afterthought or something we take for granted. We acknowledge His omnipotence in word, but the extent of that power does not always sink in or occupy our consciousness. Take a moment to sit quietly and ask God to give you insight into this. Let the Holy Spirit open your eyes to grasp how wide and long and high and deep is His loving power (Ephesians 3:18).

Unfortunately, our minds are often prone to wander, and we can easily forget whose world this is and who is in control as we go about our daily lives. We see the many tasks on our to-do list and the constant flood of entertainment and phone notifications vying for our attention. Because of this, we can forget the reality that the Lord and Creator of the universe has conquered death and set us free, and now His powerful presence lives inside His people. So it is important that we frequently stop and meditate on the loving power and presence of the Lord as He reveals Himself to us more and more.

Gospel Power

After looking at "the power of God," we are left to ask, "How does that relate to the gospel? And for us, what does it mean to be messengers of the gospel, carriers of this "power of God?" Most of us would agree that there is power in the gospel (since, you know, the Bible says so), but we don't often grasp the extent of this power, let alone see ourselves as wielders of it. We know *about* the power of the gospel, but what we need is to intimately understand and see that power as something that we carry around with us as His ambassadors. The gospel is the power of God, and that same power is also in us.

In Ephesians, there is a recurring theme of God's power and how it has been at work in the world, in the resurrection, and now at work in the Church. Ephesians 3:20–21 says, "Now to him who is able to do immeasurably more than all we ask or imagine, according to his power that is at work within us, to him be glory in the church and in Christ Jesus throughout all generations, for ever and ever! Amen."

We readily acknowledge God working in us and through us, but we rarely take seriously the extent and gravity of this. We often allow ourselves to shrink into maintenance mode as many of us are just trying to make it through the challenges of the day. Failure to appreciate God's power in us especially influences our approach to evangelism and disciple-making, causing us to enter into these opportunities with fear and trembling. Fear of people, fear of saying the wrong thing, fear of being at a loss for words or answers, fear of anything we can imagine going wrong. But God has a much greater plan and purpose. We see this, even today, as we see the gospel spreading worldwide in places and to an extent never before seen in history. The glory and the presence of God to which Paul was referring is within His people, transforming us and empowering us to do immeasurably more than we can imagine.

When Paul was talking to the Ephesians about God's power, he had in mind the Old Testament Jewish temple. God living among His people, His presence on earth, the place where heaven and earth come together: that was the temple in the Old Testament. But today, that place is us. Paul expressed this most clearly in Ephesians 2:22, where he depicted the people of God as being raised up to become a holy temple in the Lord, built up together as "a dwelling for God by his Spirit."[17] We are the place where God is living among His people, the place of God's presence on earth, the place where heaven and earth come together. It is the Holy Spirit in us!

As we discussed earlier, when we read or think back to temple stories in the Old Testament, we tend to not have difficulty imagining the power of the presence of the Lord. We think about the priests entering the holy of holies and all the precautions taken in case that person died by the overwhelming presence of God. We think about other stories like the pillar of fire and cloud leading the Israelites and the burning bush. All these stories of God's presence among His people show us the power of that presence.

We see the power of His presence most clearly in the person of Jesus, His life and ministry and, ultimately, His death and resurrection. Elsewhere in his letter to the Ephesians, Paul states:

> I pray that the eyes of your heart may be enlightened in order that you may know the hope to which he has called you, the riches of his glorious inheritance in his holy people, and his *incomparably great power for us who believe.* That power is the same as the mighty strength he exerted when he raised Christ from the dead and seated him at his right hand in the heavenly realms, far above all rule and authority, power and dominion, and every name that is invoked, not only in the present age but also in the one to come. And God placed all things under his feet and appointed him to be head over everything for the church, which is his body, the fullness of him who fills everything in every way (Ephesians 1:18–23, emphasis added).

What God has done in Christ He is doing in His church. This same power of God is in us. The same power that spoke creation into being, the same power that set the Israelites free and fed them with miraculous manna from the heavens, and the same power and presence that resided in the ark of the covenant and the tabernacle and the holy of holies. The same power that provided the Son to a virgin. The same power that raised that murdered Son from death and seated Him high above in the heavens to rule over all creation. The same power that disarmed the powers of this age making a public mockery of Satan and evil, triumphing over them on the cross (Colossians 2:15). The same power that will make all things new and bring together heaven and earth in the new creation in which He will reign for eternity. This same power is in us and in the gospel we proclaim!

As we wield this gospel of power, we are not left to wield it on our own. No, Christ has promised that He will be with us always (Matthew 28:20). Those who take up the call to engage a broken world with the gospel are promised that they can fulfill that commission with the assurance of His powerful presence and authority. We do not need to sit around and wait for His presence and power. We already have it! New Testament believers boldly stepped out in faith, proclaimed the gospel, and expected God to show up. And we can do the same.[18]

It can be hard to wrap our heads around the gospel power that is entrusted to us. Even now when I go out to share the gospel with people, I often feel self-conscious or out of place. I think to myself, *Who am I to be doing this?* There can be a sense of disconnect between biblical truth and our daily experience and feelings. This is what Paul was alluding to in 2 Corinthians 4:7 when he said, "We have this treasure in jars of clay to show that this all-surpassing power is from God and not from us." Acknowledging our own weakness as frail containers of this power of God is a good thing, but it can go too far if it keeps us from wielding that power.

When it comes to sharing the gospel, we may feel like an impostor or like it's not our place. But it absolutely is our place. This is who we are. The Holy Spirit gives us the authority and power and right to proclaim the gospel. God Almighty is the one calling us message-bearer, ambassador, evangelist, disciple-maker. How long will it take for us to be convinced that it is right and good and necessary for us to step into this role?

This power is not in us for our own sake, but for the sake of the world. As Jesus used His power to wash the feet of His disciples (John 13:1–17), we must use this power to serve and love others as well. God has always purposed to work through His people for the sake of the world. When we declare the resurrection of Christ, we tap into the same power that raised Him from the dead. That same power resides in the gospel message itself, and when we proclaim the gospel, we wield that power. For the billions of people in the world who are far from God and enslaved to sin, their primary need, above anything else we can offer them, is the gospel—to know Christ and Him crucified.

Billions of people are trapped in spiritual slavery, locked away on spiritual death row. And we, empowered by the Holy Spirit, carry around the key that unlocks the prison doors and sets the captives free to live new life in Him. That power-filled key wielded by power-filled people is God's plan to see His kingdom come and will be done on earth as it is in heaven. The gospel of Jesus Christ, the power of God for salvation, rests on our lips, waiting to be spoken to a desperate and fearful world that is enslaved to sin and blinded by Satan. We must seriously and intentionally embrace our role, our empowerment, and the purpose God has for us to set the captives free. To Him be the glory forever and ever! Amen!

Chapter Six
Expressive Aphasia

"It is written: 'I believed; therefore I have spoken.' Since we have that same spirit of faith, we also believe and therefore speak . . ."
(2 Corinthians 4:13)

"Therefore, if anyone is in Christ, the new creation has come: The old has gone, the new is here! All this is from God, who reconciled us to himself through Christ and gave us the ministry of reconciliation: that God was reconciling the world to himself in Christ, not counting people's sins against them. And he has committed to us the message of reconciliation. We are therefore Christ's ambassadors, as though God were making his appeal through us. We implore you on Christ's behalf: Be reconciled to God. God made him who had no sin to be sin for us, so that in him we might become the righteousness of God."
(2 Corinthians 5:17–21)

One morning as I started making my hospital rounds, I stepped in to see my first patient of the day. This wasn't just *any* day. This was my first day practicing medicine as a real doctor. It was simultaneously a big deal and not a big deal. Yes, it was my first day being "Dr. Porter," but at the same time I had done this thousands of times during my medical training, so it was nothing new.

When I entered the room, the nurse was talking with the patient, going over some of her medicines. As I waited for them to finish, the patient asked the nurse a question about one of her drugs. The nurse replied, "Let's see what the doctor thinks." I nodded in silent agreement that this was a good question for the doctor. After several seconds of silence, the nurse looked at me quizzically. "Dr. Porter?" "Yes?" I asked, obliviously. "What do you think about the patient's question?"

Suddenly, my new reality hit me: *I'm the doctor.* When they say, "Let's see what the doctor thinks," they want to know what *I* think. Fortunately, I could answer the question at the time, but it took much longer for me to grapple with and accept my new identity and all that it entails.

Me? Yes, You

One of the most widely recognizable passages in evangelical churches is the Great Commission, most often quoted from Matthew 28:18–20: "Then Jesus came to them and said, 'All authority in heaven and on earth has been given to me. Therefore, go and make disciples of all nations, baptizing them in the name of the Father and of the Son and of the Holy Spirit, and teaching them to obey everything I have commanded you. And surely I am with you always, to the very end of the age.'"

Despite many of us knowing this verse and even being able to recite it from heart, there is a shocking disconnect between our awareness of the Great Commission and our practice of it. To put it in terms of 2 Corinthians 4:13, we may believe it, but we ain't speaking it (that's the New Revised Texas Version). Despite some awareness of the command to share the gospel, nearly 40 percent of Christians from all age groups do not think they have a personal responsibility to share their faith.[19] A growing number of Christians, including half of millennials, actually take it a step further and say it is wrong to share your faith with a non-Christian in hopes they will become a Christian.[20] This matches and helps explain why most pastors say their congregations are particularly weak on sharing the gospel.

At the same time, spiritual openness is actually on the rise in America. As of October 2022, three out of four US adults say they want to grow spiritually, and nearly half say they are more open to God today than before the COVID pandemic. Furthermore, among non-Christians, 47 percent of teens and 36 percent of young adults said they are interested in learning more about Christianity specifically and what it could mean for their life.[21]

This is a bit of a paradox: spiritual openness is seemingly rising in America, and yet evangelism is dropping. So what is the disconnect? For starters, to be blunt, most churchgoers simply aren't interested in evangelism and discipleship. When asked to rank a list of spiritual activities that spur their excitement and interest, evangelism and discipleship ranked last behind other options like serving those in need, building community and relationships, and teaching or preaching.[22]

My question is, If you want to serve those in need, what greater need could be served than sharing the life-saving gospel with someone? If you want to build relationships, what better foundation on which to build than the gospel? If you want to teach and preach . . . you get the point.

The truth is, sharing the gospel can feel daunting and awkward. Maybe we feel unqualified or scared of how someone will respond. Or maybe we just don't feel like it is our place. Whatever the reason, of all the commands of Christ, sharing the gospel is easily the one met with the most resistance, barriers, and neglect. This should not be surprising. The gospel itself is the core of following Jesus and is the power of salvation for those who hear and believe, so it makes sense that this would be the focal point of attacks from the Enemy. Rather than unifying around the need for all believers to share the gospel, we tend to focus on our differences surrounding how, when, what, where, and with whom to share. If you ask four Christians about evangelism, you will probably get five opinions.

In medicine, we see a condition that is known as expressive aphasia. People with this diagnosis have difficulty speaking. They can understand what other people are saying, and they often know what they want to say themselves, but due to injury in the brain's speech center, they cannot express it properly. This is similar to what we see in our modern Christian culture when it comes to sharing the gospel. Despite maybe having a desire to speak or even knowing what to say, the words just don't come out. The cause of this medical problem can often be pinpointed to a specific injury such as a stroke. In our Gospel Deficiency–induced form that impedes gospel proclamation, there is a multitude of causative factors, or barriers.

We will address the various barriers to sharing the gospel in the next chapter, but first we need to answer the question posed in the Barna survey: Do all Christians have a personal responsibility to share the gospel? If that is still in question for some followers of Christ, the other barriers are irrelevant. So what does the Bible say about this?

Blessed to Bless

We see as early as Genesis that God purposed to set apart for Himself a people to be His representatives in the world. Right off the bat things start to go awry: first in the Garden of Eden and then the events leading up to the flood, followed shortly thereafter by the Tower of Babel. Humans were not off to a strong start.

From the beginning, we see that humans, in their own power, are incapable of redeeming themselves. Of course, none of this was a surprise to God.

At this point He put events in motion to set the world right. Beginning with Abraham, God promised, "I will make you into a great nation and I will bless you . . . and all people on earth will be blessed through you" (Genesis 12:2–3). God promised to bless Abraham and his family, and this family would become a blessing in the world. This is God's first direct quote following the fall, the flood, and the Tower of Babel. The plan for God to use His people to bless the nations was not an add-on or an, "Oh, and by the way . . ." that Jesus threw out there as He was about to return to heaven. This had been God's purpose since the beginning, and it has always been central to the identity of His people.

His love for all people and nations was central to His covenant with Abraham. God said that He would bless Abraham's family *so that* they could be a blessing to the entire world. This was God's beautiful rescue plan. He chose the Israelites to proclaim His kingdom in order to reconcile the entire world to Himself. We continue to see this theme running throughout the entire Old Testament. As the story unfolds, there are many twists and turns and obstacles along the way, but in the end, nothing can stand in God's way or thwart His plan.

Fast forward to the New Testament and we see this thread continuing through Jesus, His disciples, and the burgeoning early church. We see Jesus, the embodiment of a blessing to the nations, teaching and modeling the call to proclaim the good news of the kingdom of God. Everywhere He went and in everything He did, He proclaimed the kingdom of God. Whether healing or teaching or serving or even dying, He pointed people to Himself as the Savior of the world.

Jesus was teaching about His kingdom and training His disciples to make disciples throughout His entire earthly ministry. He regularly sent out His disciples to proclaim the good news (see Matthew 9:38; 28:18–20; Mark 3:14–15; 6:7–8; 16:15–18; Luke 9:1–2, 24:44–49; John 20:19–23; Acts 1:8.) In each of these passages, we see both Jesus and His disciples living into their identity as message bearers of the good news. Thus, they were fulfilling God's desire for His people to bless the nations, thereby continuing to fulfill God's initial promise to Abraham. And this, of course, continues even after Jesus' earthly ministry.

As noted earlier, with His last words in the book of Matthew, Jesus commanded His followers to "make disciples of all nations." This was a command, not a suggestion or an invitation to consider. It is a command for all people who identify themselves as followers of Christ, for all time. It is a command to actively work to lead people from lostness into a relationship with their Savior. That is the meaning of "make disciples." His followers recognized this and obediently carried out His orders.

After Jesus' ascension, His followers were filled with the Holy Spirit and immediately began proclaiming the gospel to anyone and everyone who would listen. Their identity as proclaimers of the gospel was on full display. And suddenly, thousands of people confessed Jesus as Lord. As new churches were planted, these new believers followed the disciples' example by also proclaiming the gospel widely and making disciples. Here we see the "mustard seed kingdom" manifesting in a manner just like what is described in 2 Timothy 2:2. The people of God were rapidly blessing the nations by proclaiming the gospel and making disciples, who then went and made more disciples. What better blessing could there be than introducing people to their Savior so that they might know Him and live with Him for eternity?

A Not-So-Secret Identity

Paul, playing his own integral part in the rapid expansion of the church, described the Christian identity in 2 Corinthians 5:17–21. There is a lot going on in this passage that we won't delve into but will merely focus on what Paul says are four characteristics of "anyone in Christ."

1. *Righteous/reconciled/new creation:* These are listed together because they embody the same idea. Anyone in Christ has been made new and has "become the very righteousness of God." That means that no matter what you have done or what has been done to you in the past, you are made brand new. The old is gone. When God looks at us, He sees the very righteousness of Christ.

2. *Ambassadors:* What does it mean to be an ambassador? Stop and think about the job description of an ambassador. How would you define it? What often comes to mind are things like being a representative, speaking on someone's behalf, and advocating for a certain entity, ruler, or country. That is what Paul was saying we are. We are God's representative on earth. We are here to proclaim and advocate for His kingdom.

3. *Message bearers:* Paul said that the "message of reconciliation" has been committed and entrusted to us. Verse 19 explains what this message entails: in Christ, God is reconciling and restoring His relationship with humans. This is the gospel message with which we have been entrusted to deliver to the world.

4. *Ministers:* Paul said God has given us a "ministry of reconciliation." We have the message of reconciliation, and He has

then given us a ministry, a sphere of relationships to which we are responsible to deliver that message.

In addition to seeing these individual aspects of our identity, it is important to point out that if someone is in Christ, he or she is *all* of these things. You can't be one of these things without the others. You can't pick and choose which of these you want to be or not be. Anyone who is in Christ is inherently all of these things. We may not always feel like it or display it well, but this is who we are and who we are made to be.

As you can see, points 2 through 4 all have something in common: they are related to proclaiming the good news and making disciples. This is a core piece of our identity in Christ. Sharing the gospel and making disciples is not just something we do; it is who we are. We often talk about evangelism as one ministry among many that the church offers, as we saw in the Barna survey earlier. Church members are often given the option to be involved in evangelism or not and may choose to join another ministry such as helping in the parking lot on Sunday mornings or working with the homeless ministry or helping in the nursery. All of these ministries are excellent ways to serve the church, but they are not built into the very identity of all Christians. Paul did not say, "Anyone in Christ is a new creation, and we are therefore Christ's greeters on Sunday mornings." These are ministries in which people can and should be involved, but these are things that we do, not who we are. In Christ, we are all inherently message-bearing ambassadors (i.e., evangelizers and disciple-makers). Paul here defined *all* Christians as people who represent God in the world to minister to people by bearing the message of the gospel—plain and simple.

From the beginning of creation, through to Abraham and the Israelites, to Jesus and the disciples, all the way until the new creation comes in fullness, the people of God have always been His ambassadors in the world tasked with pointing others to Him. So I will say it again: Proclaiming the good news and making disciples is not just something we do; it is who we are. It is who God has created us to be. We are not made righteous for our own good any more than Abraham and Israel were blessed for their own benefit. God blesses and bestows righteousness to His people for the purpose of blessing the nations so that His kingdom comes and expands on earth as it is in heaven.

Hopefully this quick survey of the Bible as it relates to the people of God and their role in the world clarifies any ambiguity about whether all Christians have a personal responsibility to share the gospel. Having established evangelism as inherent in the Christian identity, and seeing from the research that many people are spiritually open, what is stopping you from putting down this book right now and going to tell someone about Jesus? If the answer is, "Nothing," then toss it aside and get out there! I would love nothing more than to see this book discarded for the purpose of going out and sharing the gospel. For those who still have some roadblocks in their way, we will address those in the next chapter.

Diagnostics: Speech Therapy Evaluation

Do you know how to share the gospel in a clear, concise way? Do you feel confident about your ability to do so?

"No more people are going to be saved today than the number who hear the gospel." Do you believe this quote to be true? Why or why not? If it is true, how should that affect our day-to-day lives?

Chapter Six

Is evangelism a part of your day-to-day life? Are you regularly looking for and creating opportunities to share the gospel? Why or why not?

Do you believe that you have a personal responsibility to share the gospel with people around you who are far from God?

Does your church regularly train and equip its members in simple, reproducible ways to share the gospel?

Diagnosis: Speech impediment

Treatment

Rx: Speech therapy and excusectomy
(excising our excuses)

When we first moved to Africa, our initial task was to learn the language and culture. This was not an English-speaking country, so our options were to learn the language well or never speak to anyone ever. Learning a new language is difficult, but when you are surrounded by it and motivated by necessity, it makes it a lot easier than, say, studying Latin in high school. As anyone who has ever studied languages knows, you make a lot of embarrassing mistakes along the way. For example, I help with some administrative work at a health center where we live. As part of this, there are always documents that need to be signed and stamped. In our local language, the words used for "stamp" and "poop" sound nearly identical, at least to the untrained ear. Because of this, for the first several months working in the office, I asked a lot of people to "poop" on documents and offered to "poop" on theirs as well. The people were very gracious and gently corrected me . . . eventually.

Beginning to live into your God-given identity as a gospel messenger can feel a lot like learning a new language. You may feel timid because you don't know what to say. You may be fearful about making a mistake or being asked a question you can't answer. Just remember, God has created you for this and will be with you along the way. You will make mistakes. You will face questions you can't answer. But that's OK, because you're being obedient. Plus, mistakes aren't the end of the world. Trust me, if I can "poop" on documents and survive, so can you. Let's get to it.

Evangelism for Everyone

Once we begin to correct our gospel-deficient way of seeing people and start viewing them through Gospel Glasses in light of eternity, the enormous need for sharing the gospel will become forefront in our mind. This is a direct result of having the mind of Christ. Therefore, we must be willing to meet that gospel need and readily share with those around us. If you just got butterflies in your stomach at the prospect of intentional evangelism, you are not alone. The vast majority of Christians face major mental barriers when it comes to the dreaded "E-word." We will look at how to overcome the most common of these daunting barriers.

Evangelism is not just for the trained professionals or the specially gifted. It is nothing less than a direct command from our Lord and Savior and a key aspect of our identity in Christ. But somehow our identity and understanding of what it means to follow Jesus came unstuck from our God-given identity as ambassadors and disciple-makers. Biblically, these were two sides of the same coin. When Jesus called His disciples He said, "Follow me and I will make you fishers of men." In the same breath, Jesus commanded following and fishing to His would-be followers, and He continues to do the same today. So why is it, in the smorgasbord of Christian activities, services, and lifestyle expectations, that proclaiming the gospel is treated as optional?

We see throughout the New Testament that fishing is not only learned by following, but that it is a necessary component of following. When Jesus said, "Go and make disciples," He was talking to all Christians in all places for all time until He returns. As a command from our Lord, our failure to share the gospel and make disciples is nothing less than sinful disobedience.

Asserting that it is a sin to not share the gospel garners a lot of pushback, but what else do you call disobeying a command of Christ? Christ commands us to repent, to love, to give, to not commit murder, and so on. Would disobedience to these commands be considered anything less than sinful? Making disciples is no less a command than "Thou shall not steal," but we certainly treat it that way, don't we? "For Jesus Christ is the Lord; and thus to believe in him means at the same time a commitment to obey him."[23]

If explicit gospel proclamation to the lost is a command to be obeyed and a core aspect of living as a new creation in Christ, the onus is on us to get to it. As Robert Coleman states in his renowned book *The Master Plan of Evangelism*, "There can be no dillydallying around with the commands of Christ. We are engaged in warfare, the issues of which are life and death, and every day that we are indifferent to our responsibilities is a day lost to the cause of Christ... There is no place in the Kingdom for a slacker, for such an attitude not only precludes any growth in grace and knowledge but also destroys any usefulness on the world battlefield of evangelism."[24]

The Gospel Is Spoken

If sharing the gospel is a command to be obeyed, it is vital that we understand what it actually means to share the gospel. You have no doubt heard the quote, "Preach the gospel at all times. Use words if necessary." It is often attributed to Saint Francis of Assisi, but it turns out that he never actually said this. In fact, based on his writings he would have totally disagreed with this quote. While it's not clear where it came from, this quote and general sentiment has infiltrated contemporary Christianity like termites invade and destroy a house. It may sound nice on the surface, but it is not based on the Bible and shows a deep misunderstanding of the gospel itself.

The idea behind the quote is that proclaiming the gospel through actions is either better than using words or that somehow words are not necessary to share the gospel. There's just one problem: the gospel cannot be preached without words! Sharing the gospel is a mouth-to-ear experience; it leaves one person's mouth and travels to another person's ear. Paul explicitly contradicted the idea that words are not necessary in Romans 10:13–14: "Everyone who calls on the name of the Lord will be saved. How, then, can they call on the one they have not believed in? And how can they believe in the one of whom they have not heard? And how can they hear without someone preaching to them?"

Paul was essentially saying that people cannot come to faith in Christ without hearing the gospel. Therefore, a reliance on actions to convey the entire gospel truth reveals our misunderstanding of how the gospel actually works. In general, if we have important news to share with someone, we speak the truth plainly. We don't rely on charades and wait for them to guess what we are miming. We just tell them. Also, it's worth pointing out, Jesus found it necessary to use words. So if His actions necessitated the accompaniment of the spoken word to proclaim the good news, do we somehow think our actions speak more clearly than His?

God with Us

The good news is that we are not left to do this on our own. Jesus sent His Spirit to be with us always, and He will lead and guide the way through evangelism if we let Him. We often talk about the spirit as purifying us, teaching us, and helping us. These are all true and not to be diminished in any way. But in Acts we see an aspect of the Spirit that we often neglect, and that is the Spirit compelling believers toward seeking the salvation of those around them. For the Spirit to purify us and teach us and help us, we have no problem asking and acquiescing to this. This is no doubt our primary interest in the Holy Spirit: how He relates to and helps us. But this Spirit is a missionary Spirit seeking the salvation of the lost.

This hasn't changed or diminished since Acts, which means that it is we who are smothering the missional flame that the Spirit brings. We do this through learned behavior (inertia), mental gymnastics (rationalizing why we shouldn't share the gospel), and sin (refusing to do what we know we are commanded to), among other things. God is unchanging in His character and desire. This means that the Spirit is no less motivated to seek the salvation of the lost today than He was in the New Testament. So when we see in Acts these great missionary stories, rather than rationalizing to ourselves, "Well, maybe the Spirit doesn't work that way anymore," we need to face the facts and acknowledge that it is we the modern Christians who actually don't work that way anymore. It is not the Spirit but rather us who are slowing the spread of the gospel by withholding it from those around us.

Chapter Seven
Excising Barriers

"For though we live in the world, we do not wage war as the world does. The weapons we fight with are not the weapons of the world. On the contrary, they have divine power to demolish strongholds. We demolish arguments and every pretension that sets itself up against the knowledge of God, and we take captive every thought to make it obedient to Christ."
(2 Corinthians 10:3–5)

Clearly, there are many barriers to our sharing the gospel, so it is vitally important that we intentionally and aggressively excise them. The prescription for this is to go under the knife and surgically remove all misunderstandings, misinformation, wrongly held beliefs, and anything else poisoning our mind toward intentional evangelism. Be forewarned: there's no anesthesia for this surgery. That means it's going to be painful and difficult to get through, but you will be healthier because of it. And who knows? This procedure may even help you save someone else's life. Now, let's look at some common barriers, both internal and external, that need to be removed.

Internal Barriers

Inertia
A rudimentary definition of inertia is "objects at rest tend to stay at rest, and objects in motion tend to continue in the same mo-

tion, unless acted upon by an outside force." We see this in many facets of life, not least of all in our churches and ministries. Basically, we are prone to maintain the status quo. Our lack of engagement in evangelism often boils down to the fact that we aren't already doing it, so we just continue not doing it. It's not part of our routine, so we don't think about it. Whether it is church tradition, neglect, or just plain laziness, the most natural course is to keep doing the same things we have always been doing. As the definition states, for this to change it must be acted upon by an outside force. That outside force may come in the form of direct intervention by the Holy Spirit, a friend, a preacher, or maybe even reading a mediocre book on the topic. Whatever it may be, things are likely to stay the same unless conscious, intentional action is taken.

Therefore, for those people and churches who find themselves in this position and see the need for change, the first step is prayer. Ask the Lord to provide for you a way to move forward. He provides for those He calls, and you are called. He will not call you to a task without providing everything you need to accomplish it. Not only that, but He will provide what you need to get started, that "outside force" to get you moving in the right direction. When we pray for things like this, He is faithful to provide, so as soon as you start praying, be on the lookout for His answer.

Second, look for people and churches who are engaging in the harvest to make disciples, and learn from them. Ask for training or resources or even just go watch what they are doing. Observing someone perform a task provides more instruction than talking or reading about it ever could.

Busyness

When I ask people what keeps them from intentionally engaging others with the gospel, the most common response is, "I don't have enough time." Now, I will admit that I don't actually believe that busyness is the most common barrier. Staying busy and then talking about how busy we are is becoming more and more prevalent in our culture. Therefore, it is an easier and more socially acceptable barrier to admit as opposed to others. But even though this barrier seems exceedingly common, it is actually one of the most straightforward to confront.

If we say we are "too busy" to share the gospel and engage in the work of making disciples, this is an indication that we don't understand our calling to be disciple-makers. We fill our time with lots of things every day, and for Christians, a lot of these things may be very good, God-honoring things. I don't doubt that most Christians sincerely desire to spend their time doing what honors their Father. But if our schedule is too full of "good things" to make disciples, we must not understand our calling. If we truly understood that sharing the gospel and making disciples is a command from our King, surely we would make time for it, right? This explanation for busyness is giving people the benefit of the doubt that they are truly trying to honor God with their time but simply do not know that they are called to be disciple-makers. In this case, once we understand and embrace this call, we must learn when to say no to "good things" so we can say yes to better things. Or, stated differently, we must learn to say no to optional things so we can say yes to commanded things.

Fear of Man

Whether we recognize it or not, many of us suffer from what I call "fear of man syndrome." Symptoms of this condition may include excessive concern of what others think about you, frequently second-guessing your decisions because of the possibility of being poorly perceived by people, being driven to please others or live up to their expectations, and compulsively checking your likes on social media posts, among others. One reason some of us don't share the gospel is because we are afraid of what people might think or that they won't like what we have to say. Maybe it's not politically correct to talk about faith, and we don't want to ruffle any feathers.

There is no shortage of Bible characters who dealt with this as well, so if you find yourself stuck behind this barrier, you are not alone. Here are a few examples:

Saul, king of Israel

"Then Saul said to Samuel, 'I have sinned. I violated the Lord's command . . . I was afraid of the men and so I gave in to them'" (1 Samuel 15:24).

Jewish religious leaders who believed in Jesus

"Even after Jesus had performed so many signs in their presence, they still would not believe in him. . . . Yet at the same time many even among the leaders believed in him. But because of the Pharisees they would not openly acknowledge their faith for fear they would be put out of the synagogue; for they loved human praise more than praise from God" (John 12:37, 42–43).

Peter, then Barnabas, and other Christians

"When [Peter] came to Antioch, [Paul] opposed him to his face, because he stood condemned. For before certain men came from James, he used to eat with the Gentiles. But when they arrived, he began to draw back and separate himself from the Gentiles because he was afraid of those who belonged to the circumcision group. The other Jews joined him in his hypocrisy, so that by their hypocrisy even Barnabas was led astray" (Galatians 2:11–13).

When you start down this list, at first you see Saul and might think, *Yeah, I could see that he was far from perfect.* Second, you see the Jewish religious leaders and think, *Sure that makes sense because they had a lot of baggage and other issues going on.* But then you get to the third point and see Peter, Barnabas, and many others in the early church. Wait, what? Even Peter? The same guy who led thousands to Christ at Pentecost, and walked on water with Jesus, and had a vision directly from the Lord showing him to accept the Gentiles? That Peter? Yep, apparently so. On top of that, while you might expect some growing pains in the early church as they worked out the kinks and figured out what this new way of living looked like, this scene happened at least twelve years (likely more) after Jesus' ascension! Which means that Peter, "the rock," was still struggling with fear of man in the midst of seeing the amazing works of Jesus and the Holy Spirit. If it could happen to him, it can happen to all of us.

Just as the Bible has many examples of people suffering from Fear of Man Syndrome, it also has many verses aimed at combatting it:

Proverbs 29:25

"Fear of man will prove to be a snare, but whoever trusts in the Lord is kept safe."

Psalm 118:8

"It is better to take refuge in the LORD than to trust in humans."

Galatians 1:10

"Am I now trying to win the approval of human beings, or of God? Or am I trying to please people? If I were still trying to please people, I would not be a servant of Christ."

Colossians 3:23-24

"Whatever you do, work at it with all your heart, as working for the Lord, not for human masters, since you know that you will receive an inheritance from the Lord as a reward. It is the Lord Christ you are serving."

The list of verses speaking against the fear of man could go on for several pages, but you get the point. Fear of man = bad. Trust in the Lord = good. Pretty straightforward. However, while this lesson is simple, that doesn't mean it's easy. This is an affliction that only God can take away, so if we deal with this, even a little, we must ask the Lord to rescue us. As long as we are seeking to please people, we cannot fully please our Lord.

"I Don't Know What to Say"

Maybe we recognize that we should share the gospel and have a desire to, but we just don't know how. What do we even say to start that conversation? "Hey friend, how's your family? How's work? How do you feel about spending eternity in hell?" Probably not.

There are a lot of reasons people face this barrier. For me, it was that I grew up in churches that did not equip us to share the gospel in a simple, understandable, culturally appropriate way. I knew all about Jesus and the Bible, but I didn't have a simple way to clearly communicate the good news. The sad reality of the contemporary Western church is that this is exceedingly common.

When I lived in the United States, I had the privilege of leading what we call Gospel Conversations Training at several local churches. Before the actual training began, I met with pastors to discuss the training content and evaluate the needs of their church. Two questions I always asked in these meetings were, "Are your members equipped to and comfortable with sharing the gospel? And are there church members who are actively and consistently sharing and making disciples?" I cannot remember a single pastor who answered positively or enthusiastically to these questions. Without fail, they almost always answered "no" to both. Many will say that generic outreach or community engagement are strengths, but I haven't met many pastors—or Christians, for that matter—who identify gospel communication as a strength.

So how do we remedy this? In these training events, we addressed this barrier by training people in simple, reproducible gospel-sharing tools. The best tools are (1) simple enough to communicate in a clear, concise way (think: no more than two to three minutes) and (2) reproducible so that the hearer is able to repeat it to others. That being said, it is always important to point out that there is no magic in any given tool. The power is in the gospel, not the tool. The important thing is for people to have one or two gospel-sharing tools in their tool belt that they know well and feel comfortable using. There are lots of good tools out there that can be easily found online, but a few of the most widely used and effective (in terms of clarity and simplicity) ones are the three circles, one-minute testimony (aka God's story/my story), and the bridge illustration. Each has its strengths and weaknesses, and some are better for certain populations and situations, so it is necessary for each person to find what works for them.

In addition to finding a simple, reproducible gospel-sharing tool to use, it is essential to practice. Practice, practice, and then practice again. This way, when the time comes and the Holy Spirit prompts you to share with someone or your coworker is struggling and feeling hopeless and needs to hear the good news, that voice in your head saying, "I don't know what to say," will be squashed. With enough practice, you will have the confidence to know you will get the gospel right, even if you stumble awkwardly through the rest of the conversation.

Any time I lead a disciple-making training, a large portion of the time is spent learning and practicing gospel-sharing tools. Then after sufficient practice, we put the tools to use. We divide up into groups of two or three and walk around the surrounding area to pray with people and share the gospel. During one such training at a local church, I teamed up with two guys who seemed rather timid and unsure of themselves. As we went out, I started the first few conversations and shared with those people. Unfortunately, none of the people I shared with that day were receptive, and they each declined to continue talking. Then, having seen me do it a few times, it came time for one of the trainees to give it a shot. Chris was the first guy up. He was clearly nervous, but there was no turning back at this point.

As we encountered the next person in the neighborhood, there was a long moment of silence until Chris finally started talking. He stumbled right out of the gate, having trouble explaining what we were doing or why we were out in this neighborhood to begin with. He even momentarily forgot the name of his church that sent us out. It was rough. Fortunately, the guy who was listening remained polite and attentive. Despite all of Chris's difficulties, the one part of the conversation that actually went well was the gospel sharing (because he had practiced!). He clearly and succinctly presented one of the simple tools from the training. And wouldn't you know it, the guy listening not only understood Chris's gospel presentation, but on top of that he wanted to meet again to learn more about following Jesus!

Of all the interactions we had that evening, the only person who responded positively was the guy with whom Chris shared. This was an important lesson for all of us. As we saw, the power was not in the presentation, the wording, or the smoothness of the conversation. The power is in the gospel. As long as the gospel is communicated, God can and will use it. Sure, my conversations and presentations might have been more polished and smooth, but that didn't matter. Chris accurately communicated the gospel, and that was enough. The Holy Spirit had prepared Chris's listener to hear and respond to the gospel, so when that gospel seed landed, the soil was ready to accept it and start growing. The take-home point is this: find a simple, reproducible gospel-sharing tool with which you feel comfortable, practice it, pray for opportunities to use it, and trust the Holy Spirit to take care of the rest.

Gospel Confidence

We may know that we need to share and we may know what to share, but we lack confidence. When the time comes, we get cold feet and put it off until later. Like most things in life, the trick to building up confidence in evangelism comes from practice and getting out and doing it. Michael Jordan didn't roll out of bed one day and decide to be the most dominant, fearless athlete in his sport. He spent his entire life dribbling, shooting, practicing, competing, and so on. Then when he got the ball in his hands and time was running out and the championship was on the line, he knew he was going to make the game-winning shot. There was no question in his mind. That's confidence.

Just like practicing basketball techniques, practicing gospel conversations can help build up confidence. By intentionally practicing your chosen gospel-sharing tool and rehearsing how you get into and out of these conversations, you will gain confidence so that when the time comes you will be ready. Grab a friend, family member, or even your pet and practice sharing the gospel with them. Have your human partners ask you follow-up questions or give different responses or scenarios. If you're not confident in sharing the gospel in a practice setting, you likely won't be in a real-life scenario. So if you want to "be like Mike," then, as his sponsors say, "Just do it!"

A different form of the confidence barrier is not so much lack of confidence in yourself as it is lack of confidence in evangelism in general. It's easy to scoff at the idea of evangelism and assume it's pointless, either because you believe the hearer won't be interested or because you have never seen effective evangelism. We discussed the power of the gospel in depth previously, but to reiterate, we must place our confidence in the Holy Spirit and the power of the gospel. The Holy Spirit is the one who changes hearts (John 16:8–11) and removes Satan's blinders from the eyes of the lost (2 Corinthians 4:4–6). The gospel is the power of God for salvation (Romans 1:16). Our job is to be obedient, not to achieve a certain outcome. So we obediently share the gospel and leave the results to God. We do our job and trust Him to do His.

Gifting

"I don't have the gift of evangelism." Have you ever thought this or heard others express a similar sentiment? If I had a nickel for every time someone told me that the reason they don't share the gospel with people is because of a lack of gifting, well, I'd have a lot of nickels. This is a surprisingly common response in certain church and denominational circles. There has been a renewed focus on biblical gifting and the affirming of unique gifts within the Western church in recent years, which, when staying within the biblical lanes, is a good thing. But for some, this idea of biblical gifting has gone too far in the other direction to the point that some people think that they are only responsible for their areas of gifting. This often translates into people thinking that they are not responsible for, and therefore, do not get involved in, ministries or activities for which they do not feel a special gifting.

We could spend a whole chapter analyzing the cultural psychology and philosophy behind this phenomenon including everything from postmodern influences to Western individualism, but let's skip all that and go straight to what the Bible says about it. As we have seen, all Christians are called to be disciple-makers and ambassadors for Christ (2 Corinthians 5:17–21). And all Christians are called to share the gospel, which is the same as saying all Christians are called to evangelism. In light of this truth, there are two options: (1) God provides all that we need to share the gospel and make disciples, and this does not require special gifting, or (2) God has called us all to something but has failed to give us what we need to obediently carry out this calling. I'm in the camp of the first option.

This means that a "lack of gifting" for evangelism is not a valid reason to ignore or neglect sharing the gospel. In fact, this sentiment is really nothing more than a pseudo-spiritualized excuse for disobedience to the Great Commission. Think about how you would respond if someone in your church said, "I don't have the gift of giving, so I'm not going to give to the church or to people in need anymore. I'll leave that to the gifted givers." We would never let someone get away with that! What if someone said the same thing about the gift of mercy (Romans 12:8) or faith (1 Corinthians 12:9)?

There is a general consensus in the Western church that all Christians are called to give, have faith, and show mercy. And while some have a particular gifting in these areas, all Christians are expected to manifest them in some measure. The difference is that there is not a general recognition that all Christians are called to evangelize. If we are being honest, most of us don't want to be involved in evangelism. It is hard, uncomfortable, and culturally awkward. Rather than admit that, though, we chalk it up to a lack of gifting and move on to a different ministry.

The idea that evangelism is only for the gifted must be confronted with biblical truth until sharing the gospel is recognized as a call for all. Biblical truth is the only scalpel to remove this barrier. Recognizing our joint call to evangelism as followers of Christ and helping others see this is a big step toward awakening the entire Bride of Christ to the Great Commission and treating Gospel Deficiency.

What If . . . ?

For some people, it's not the sharing the gospel part that's the problem so much as the uncertainty about what comes after. What if the listener ask a question you can't answer? What if they argue against Christianity, and you can't respond adequately? Or what if they say yes and give their life to Christ, and you don't know what to do next? We can play the what-if game all day to the point that we are either ruled by fear or think we must have a response for every conceivable scenario figured out before we step one foot out the door. Both of these usually result in a failure to go at all.

This is not too dissimilar to what many physicians face in medical training. Throughout my seven-year journey through medical school and residency, I often found myself dwelling on what I might get wrong or if I would ever be fully prepared to practice on my own or what to do if a patient asked me a question that I couldn't answer. But showing up at the hospital each day was not optional. Of course there were times when I didn't know what to do or faced a question I couldn't answer, but in training I was surrounded by more experienced people who could help. And together, we figured things out.

The same thing happened when I began intentionally setting out to work toward making disciples. My first experience in street evangelism was in an inner-city neighborhood that was known for gun violence, drugs, and crime. During that time, I experienced everything from rejection, to difficult questions, to getting sucked into listening to the latest conspiracy theories, to being offered drugs, to being propositioned by prostitutes, to being asked to answer for the rampant racism in America, and much more. However, during this time, I also saw entire households come to Christ and people turn away from their life of drugs and prostitution to follow Jesus.

You will never be fully prepared to answer every what-if scenario, but this is a beautiful opportunity to trust and surrender to the Lord. It's an opportunity to walk out in faith expecting that He will show up. If you are asked hard questions, take it to the Lord. If you don't know how to disciple a new believer, find a partner to help and train you. Find books or websites that provide training for discipleship. God has called us to make disciples, and He will provide everything we need to accomplish the task He has given us.

Rather than asking these sort of what-if questions, we should replace these thoughts with "because God" statements. Because God wants to see His kingdom come on earth as in heaven, He has called me to make disciples. Because God has called me to make disciples, I trust that He will equip me to do so. Because

God so loved the world, He sent Jesus, whom we proclaim as Lord and Savior. Because God wills that none should perish and there are people around me who are far from him and walking a road that leads to hell, I will forgo my fears and take responsibility for sharing the gospel with them. Perhaps the only what-if question we should be asking ourselves is, "What if I don't go?"

Unqualified

Some of us may think sharing the gospel is something reserved for trained pastors and clergy. "I'm not qualified to do that. I didn't go to seminary," you might say. Some of us may have even been raised in a church culture that emphasized a high power distance, meaning that the leaders were put up on a pedestal and held all the power and scriptural authority while parishioners were down below and spiritually dependent on them. Whatever the underlying reason, some people feel as if they do not have the necessary education or training or status to make disciples.

While pastors, leaders, teachers, elders, and so on are all to be respected for their God-ordained position and responsibility within the church, they are not the only ones who have responsibilities within the body of Christ. When it comes to sharing the gospel and making disciples, all Christians share that responsibility. We are all called to this, and God equips those He calls.

Throughout the New Testament, we see regular Christians, not just Apostles, out sharing the gospel, making disciples, and even planting churches. Many of these are relative unknowns (historically) like Epaphras, who planted the church among the Colossians (Colossians 1:7); Tychicus, who helped train and encourage the Ephesian church (Ephesians 6:21–22); and Philip, who pioneered in an unreached part of Samaria, was then called by the Holy Spirit to the desert, and baptized an Ethiopian, who was the first recorded African Christian in the Bible (Acts 8). The list could go on. By many of our standards today, these men would have been unqualified too. But they understood and embraced the priesthood of believers (1 Peter 2:5) and their responsibility to make disciples.

God has been using regular men and women to proclaim His kingdom and lead people to Christ since the beginning, and He continues to do this today. Most of the largest movements to Christ around the world right now, some of which are seeing hundreds of thousands of new believers come to Christ, are being led by lay Christians who never stepped foot in seminary. The only way these huge movements can happen is if all believers, young and old, educated and uneducated, rich and poor, embrace their God-given task to make disciples and trust God to equip them. And we must do the same. Because ultimately, it's not just your pastor's job to reach your city. It's yours.

Sin

Among all the barriers we have discussed, we have seen that they commonly fall into one of three categories: calling (either misunderstood or unrecognized), competence or know-how, and confidence. But apart from these, the one barrier we have not discussed, which is in a category all on its own, is sin. Yep, this is about to get uncomfortable.

By definition, sin implies acting in opposition to God's will, or disobeying Him. If He wills that His kingdom would come on earth as it is in heaven and has purposed to use us toward this end by giving us the Great Commission, what else would you call our failure to obey? Disobeying the Great Commission and our call to share the gospel is, by definition, sin. For most of us, this isn't a knowing and willful act of disobedience, but rather a product of these other barriers. Whatever the reason, lack of obedience or even delayed obedience is disobedience.

Think of it this way: If your boss at work told you to do something and you didn't do it, how do you think that would go over? For most of us, our job at work is whatever our boss says it is, and they expect us to follow orders. Most good bosses will have grace for misunderstanding an assignment or the need for assistance or more training to accomplish a task, but they still expect the job to get done. Likewise, good employees listen to their boss and do their best to accomplish the tasks set before them. If we honor the will of our earthly bosses, how much more should we honor the will of our heavenly Boss?

Thankfully, our God is full of grace and mercy and compassion, abounding in love (Nehemiah 9:17) as we all work out what it means to faithfully follow Him (Philippians 2:12). Whatever barriers we face, we trust that "there is now no condemnation for those in Christ Jesus" (Romans 8:1). If through this study we discover that we need more training or need to trust God more or even that we are just plain-and-simple sinful people, whatever it is, God still loves us and desires a relationship with us (John 3:16–18). After all, He is the one who, being "rich in mercy made us alive with Christ even when we were dead in our transgressions" (Ephesians 2:4–5), and He is the one who died for us while we were still sinners (Romans 5:8).

We must remember that we are His children, and He lavishes His love on us (1 John 3:1). As a good Father, He can handle our shortcomings. He can handle our troubles, our scars, our slowness to obey, our lack of understanding, and even our sin. And He handles them all with grace and love. So if at this point you are feeling discouraged or hopeless or are stuck behind a seemingly insurmountable barrier, take heart! If you are faithful to let Him, God, who began a good work in you, is faithful to complete it (Philippians 1:6).

External Barriers

In the previous section, all of the barriers that were addressed were essentially internal. From lack of confidence to fear to sin, these are all gospel-sharing barriers within ourselves. But we also might face external barriers. These external roadblocks fall into two categories of opposition: (1) other people and (2) Satan and the powers of evil. Let's first look at opposition from other people.

Interpersonal Conflict

In any given town to which Jesus, Paul, Peter, and the other disciples traveled, there were often people who heard and believed the good news. There were also plenty of people who rejected this good news, often with hostility. Jesus tells us to expect this (John 15:18–21), and we also see many biblical examples of this playing out.

When Jesus or His followers engaged people with the good news of the kingdom, we immediately see the gospel bringing division, as Jesus said it would in Matthew 10:34–39. (See also Hebrews 4:12.) It is important to note that in Matthew 10, when Jesus was describing this inevitable division that will occur, it is in the context of Him sending out His disciples to proclaim the good news. When the gospel is presented, it causes division. Jesus experienced this Himself too, not only in the crucifixion, but in the many stories of Him facing opposition to His message.

We often think about division, particularly in families or close relationships, as a terrible thing to be avoided at all costs. Granted, division within the church or severed relationships in any sphere of life are never to be desired or sought after: "As far as it depends on you live at peace with everyone" (Romans 12:18). But the message of the gospel is inherently polarizing. And that's the point. Not to intentionally cause tension in relationships but to reveal who is ready to give up their lives and follow Jesus. It is calling people away from one kingdom, one allegiance, and one way of living and into a wholly different life. This immediately puts all hearers into one of two camps: those who hear and believe and those who hear and reject. Dividing the whole world into two categories is, by definition, polarizing and dividing. That's the nature of the gospel.

In 1 Corinthians 1:23, Paul sums up the radical nature of the gospel nicely by calling it a "stumbling block" and "foolishness" to those outside the church. The Greek word translated "stumbling block" is *skandalon*, from which we derive our word *scandal*. Calling the gospel a "scandal" or "scandalous" is actually more in line with the original meaning of the text. The original word used for "foolishness" is *moria*, from which we derive our words *moron* and *moronic*. So in the world's eyes, we are scandalous morons when we follow Christ and share the gospel. Who wouldn't want to sign up for that?

As we embrace our identity as ambassadors of Christ and engage people with the gospel, we will face rejection along the way. Some of our closest relationships may be stressed. Maintaining healthy relationships is a good, God-honoring thing. The value of relationships, however, cannot be placed above the value of salvation, eternal life, and freedom from slavery to sin and death. We often think of polarizing topics as something to be avoided and that the loving thing to do is to keep the peace and not talk about our differences. In many cases, that may be appropriate, but the good news of Jesus Christ is different. It is not loving to not talk about it with people who are far from God. The most loving thing you can do is to tell people about their Savior. The question we must ask ourselves is this: Do we love people enough to risk our relationship with them for the sake of their salvation?

There is one huge caveat in all of this: it is one thing for interpersonal conflict to come from the gospel itself, but it is an entirely different matter if the conflict comes from how we share the gospel. We can expect that some people will be angered and offended by the gospel news itself. That is inevitable. But they should not be angered and offended by us. If our behavior, attitude, or method of gospel sharing is what turns people away, we have failed and missed the point. It all comes back to love, right? We share the gospel because we love people and want to see them enter into a loving relationship with the Lord. Therefore, our methods of sharing the gospel must also be rooted in love. The gospel is inherently offensive and scandalous. We shouldn't be.

Spiritual Conflict

The kingdom of God manifests itself differently now than it will in the future. We know that God's kingdom will come in fullness in new creation, but right now, it's easy to see that we aren't there yet. Elements of the kingdom of God have entered into the world (Mark 1:15), but elements of evil still exist. In Matthew 13:24–30, 36–43, Jesus tells the kingdom parable of the wheat and the weeds depicting this time when good and bad occupy the same area. This inevitably leads to conflict between competing forces. Jesus is growing His people on earth to produce a kingdom harvest while Satan tries to disrupt this by sowing his own evil seed. The kingdom of God is a present spiritual reality that will one day cover the earth as the waters cover the sea (Isaiah 11:9). On that day, evil will be removed completely. Until then, we must be prepared to face it.

The Bible calls Satan "the god of this age" (2 Corinthians 4:4), the "prince of this world" (John 12:31), and "the ruler of the kingdom of the air" (Ephesians 2:2). He is also known as the adversary, tempter, destroyer, accuser, liar, thief, and murderer. Quite the résumé. His goal is to lead people away from the loving presence and knowledge of God. He has been at it since the beginning in the garden. In Genesis 3, we see that he questioned God's word (v. 1), he denied God's word (v. 4), and he distorted God's word (v. 5). He continues to use these tactics on the people of God to this day.

He even had the audacity to try his deceitful schemes on God Himself, tempting Jesus in the desert (Luke 4:1–13; Matthew 4:1–11). In this temptation narrative, Satan again tried to derail the purposes of God and went back to the same old playbook from the garden by questioning and distorting God's word. Of course, Jesus didn't fall for any of this, and He fought back as the Word of God using the word of God.

Christ was victorious in this battle, and soon after this He sealed His victory in the war. Christ came to "destroy the devil's work" (1 John 3:8), and the death blow was delivered through the cross and resurrection. Satan now stands condemned (John 16:11). By His death, Jesus has broken the power of Him who holds the power of death—that is, the devil—and has freed those who all their lives were held in slavery by their fear of death (Hebrews 2:14–15). So we rejoice and hold fast to this reality when we encounter spiritual conflict.

During this period of time, Satan, the defeated foe, will continue to cause trouble in this world until God's kingdom comes in fullness and all evil is vanquished for eternity. For now, the people of God in general—and especially the ones engaged in sharing the gospel and making disciples—will face focused attacks from Satan, as will new believers who come to Christ through the power of the gospel: "All believers are marked targets for attack from the same enemies that oppose and attack the person, plans, and purposes of God."[25]

The work of gospel proclamation is a particular area under constant attack from the enemy. Think about it: We are storming the gates of hell (Matthew 16:18), entering enemy territory (Ephesians 2:2), and reclaiming it for our King (1 John 5:4). This is the absolute last thing Satan wants, and he will fight back with all he has. Thanks be to God that He has given us His Spirit to wage this battle. We have the armor of God, and we must put it on daily (Ephesians 6:10–13).

Spiritual warfare is a reality we must face. The daily defeat of our enemy depends on our reliance on the word of God and the person and work of our Lord Jesus Christ. Christ gave Himself for our sins to rescue us from the present evil age (Galatians 1:4). Now we are free from the power of evil and able to walk in God's glorious light and illuminate the path to salvation for others.

Over time, when spiritual warfare inevitably starts to weigh on us and we feel discouraged, just remember: the triumph of Christ has already begun! God accomplished the first stage in His redemptive work in the death and resurrection of Christ. Satan's power has been broken, and now we may know the rule of God in our lives. We are living in the beginning of the triumph but are waiting for it to come to full fruition when all of creation will yield to His rule. During this intervening time, there will be conflict as these kingdoms collide. We represent a foreign invading kingdom in enemy territory. This is the world in which we find ourselves, and we have a distinct role to play. When we engage in gospel proclamation, we are the tip of the spear in the great battle to redeem all of creation.

Chapter Eight
Autoimmune Disorder

"Finally, brothers and sisters, rejoice! Strive for full restoration, encourage one another, be of one mind, live in peace. And the God of love and peace will be with you. . . . May the grace of the Lord Jesus Christ, and the love of God, and the fellowship of the Holy Spirit be with you all."
(2 Corinthians 13:11, 14)

"If you don't fix this, you're gonna die." Charlie had recently moved to a new city to serve as pastor at a local church. The church members had been warm and welcoming, and he was excited to begin this new journey. As is typically the case for new pastors, he looked for new and creative ways to spice things up and bring some new life into this dwindling congregation. One of those initiatives was to rearrange and update the sanctuary to look a bit more modern. He replaced creaking pews with chairs, installed new speakers, and removed the American and Christian flags that were commonplace in older churches.

Despite the legacy nature of the church, the congregation accepted the new chairs and the new speakers, as long as they weren't too loud. It wasn't until he removed the flags that he received some pushback. Many of the congregants were veterans and took great pride in attending a church that honored the country they fought for. Initially, the pastor explained his reasoning for removing the flag and declined to give in: "Not only are we updating the sanctuary to be more modern, we also want to make it clear that our focus is on Christ and not the world." That explanation wasn't good enough. The next Sunday, Charlie entered the sanctuary to find the American flag back in its place of prominence.[26]

After several weeks of back and forth, Charlie continued to stand his ground on the issue. That is, until he walked out to get his mail one day to find this note in his mailbox. The note made it clear that his life was under threat unless the American flag remained in the sanctuary. Soon thereafter, Charlie left that church.

A Body of One

We began the assessment of Gospel Deficiency by looking at how the gospel affects us personally. This was the focus of the early chapters about body odor and pica. From there we extrapolated the effects of an inward deficiency. The first was myopia (nearsightedness), a lack of eternal vision. From there it was on to impotence (a perceived lack of gospel power) and aphasia (our inability or refusal to verbally proclaim the gospel). This progression shows how the gospel spreads by taking root in our hearts, growing, and then reaping a harvest in the outside world.

However, each of these symptoms focus largely on the individual Christian. While many symptoms of Gospel Deficiency manifest within an individual or in one person's actions toward another, it can also manifest within the body of believers. Rather than an isolated disease, it develops into a corporate epidemic. And when this epidemic causes the body to attack itself, it is particularly deadly.

In medicine, there is a category of illnesses we refer to as *autoimmune diseases*. The hallmark feature of this category is that the body attacks itself. The immune system, which is designed to fight off harmful intruding pathogens, develops a misplaced focus on fighting healthy parts of its own body. One part of the body picks fights with another part of the body, destroying itself in the process. The very thing the immune system was meant to serve and protect becomes its enemy.

A similar phenomenon occurs when Gospel Deficiency invades a corporate body of believers. Instead of the local and global Church working together to love and serve each other, to encourage and build up one another, it can turn on itself by attacking its own members and dividing along ideological or preferential lines.

Intrachurch tension and division is nothing new. In many cases, Paul's letters emphasize unity among believers because of some problem or disagreement that arose within the church. That is what we see in his letters to the Corinthians. They were dealing with everything from incest to idolatry, power struggles, and gender issues, among other things. When Paul addressed these problems, the Corinthians resorted to attacking Paul himself. And this was in a place where Acts 18 tells us he stayed for a year and a half. Contrast this to other places like the Thessalonian church, where he only spent about three weeks (Acts 17:2). The Corinthians had ample time to learn from and about Paul, and yet they were plagued with more problems than most other churches he planted.

Paul was constantly reminding the Corinthians, and other churches, that in Christ, no one is an island. We are part of a new family and new community: the people of God. To demonstrate the unity we have in Christ, Paul used the body analogy. In 1 Corinthians 12:12–14, Paul says, "Just as a body, though one, has many parts, but all its many parts form one body, so it is with Christ. For we were all baptized by one Spirit so as to form one body—whether Jews or Gentiles, slave or free—and we were all given the one Spirit to drink. Even so the body is not made up of one part but of many." Likewise, Romans 12:4–5 says, "For just as each of us has one body with many members, and these members do not all have the same function, so in Christ we, though many, form one body, and each member belongs to all the others." We previously discussed our identity in Christ as His ambassadors and righteous, reconciled, new creations. But another aspect inherent to our identity in Christ is that we become a part of one body: the Church.

Unity versus Division

Churches today may or may not be dealing with the same issues as the Corinthians, but as sinful, broken people, we never cease to find things to fight about. Over the last few years, more and more pastors have expressed concern about growing divisions within their church. Many surveys demonstrate that disunity within the body is many pastors' biggest struggle.

We have seen that attacks on church unity are nothing new, but what is causing this recent uptick of church infighting? What is causing the body to turn on itself like a diseased immune system? What are the common points of conflict?

The issues that tend to be the focus of these divisions are sociopolitical issues. The content of the disagreements is not surprising since people all over the country and around the world are increasingly polarized by these same arguments. The only surprising thing is that, when it comes to these issues, our churches often act and react identically to those outside the church. Maybe the opinions are different, but the same worldly response is present. Rather than acting like a chosen people who are set apart *from* the world (1 Peter 2:9), many of us are set on being a part *of* the world. In the past, church divisions were largely based around theology, worship styles, and interpersonal disagreements. Now, the fault lines tend to form around political ideology and cultural values. And it's not just individual churches who are dealing with this either. Several denominations have split over these same issues, and there are others whose cracks are showing more and more each day. Many prominent church and denominational leaders are leaving or being forced to leave because of differing opinions about these nonsalvation issues.

As I have stated throughout this book, the focus here is not on the merits or particulars of these specific issues. Rather, the focus is, and should be for all of us, on elevating Christ and His gospel to its proper place over and above everything else—for Christ to be our utmost priority and focus and defining attribute.

Diagnostics

In autoimmune disorders, we often see an elevation of something called *inflammatory markers*. These are specific measurables on bloodwork that can tell the doctor how much inflammation is in your body to determine if it's reacting to something. What are some inflammatory markers in your church? What are some specific things you can measure to determine how inflammatory your church is? Some options include surveying the congregation about the following:

> What are some extrabiblical, strongly held beliefs and to what lengths they are willing to go to defend those beliefs?
>
> What type of people should or shouldn't be welcomed into the church and why?
>
> Are they able to work, worship, and learn with people who disagree with them about sociopolitical issues?
>
> What makes them angry, and what is an appropriate response to that anger?

Chapter Eight

These are just a few examples based on this chapter, but you know yourself and your congregation best. Pray through this and come up with your own measurable inflammatory markers.

Inflammation itself is not inherently bad. In fact, it is a natural body response aimed at helping the body heal or fight off a foreign invader. The problem comes when the inflammation is misplaced. Paul says our battle is not against other people (Ephesians 6:12), so when we battle against other people, that is misplaced inflammation. Who are you battling against? Are your time and energy and thoughts spent more on battling against flesh and blood or battling against Satan and the principalities and powers, the spiritual forces of evil?

Unity within the church is one of the most consistently taught values in the New Testament. Does the focus of your sermons, studies, and so on reflect that? Do any worldly values get more time and attention in your church than this? Are you an agent of unity or an agent of division in your church?

Diagnosis: Self-destructive tendencies

Treatment

Rx: Guard the Unity

A well-known maxim among missionaries is, "The number-one reason missionaries leave the field is because of other missionaries." In my experience, this is also true for ministers and church members who often leave their ministry or church because of other Christians. This might seem astonishing at first, but when you put a bunch of sinful people together in close proximity, conflict is inevitable. We have different ideas, personalities, and ways of doing things. And that is OK! As Paul discussed throughout

1 Corinthians, differences exist within the church because the Holy Spirit has created us differently. But when we focus on our differences, rather than the One who unites us, problems arise.

Paul went on to point out to the Corinthian church that the Holy Spirit was the author of their unity and also the author of their diversity. As Christians, we are all unified in one Spirit and part of one body in Christ. We are also each uniquely created and must faithfully embrace that diversity to bring glory to God. We are called to unity, not uniformity.

In Ephesians 4, Paul expounds on the unity we have in Christ:

> As a prisoner for the Lord, then, I urge you to live a life worthy of the calling you have received. Be completely humble and gentle; be patient, bearing with one another in love. Make every effort to keep the unity of the Spirit through the bond of peace. There is one body and one Spirit, just as you were called to one hope when you were called; one Lord, one faith, one baptism; one God and Father of all, who is over all and through all and in all. (Ephesians 4:1–6)

Paul merged together the idea of living a life "worthy of the calling you have received" with humility, gentleness, and patience. He called the church to bear with one another in love at all times, but this is especially important in times of conflict. There was a lot of conflict within the Corinthian church, and Paul addressed this by pointing them back to love and unity. This is what it means for the people of God to do life together in a manner worthy of the calling of the Lord, to live a life worthy of the gospel of Christ (Philippians 1:27).

This passage in Ephesians from the NIV translates verse 3 as "keep the unity," but other translations use "guard" or "protect" the unity. The implication here is that unity among the body of believers already exists. We do not have to establish unity or manufacture unity or increase unity. As followers of Christ, we *are* unified in the Spirit. The trouble comes when this unity is stressed, strained, attacked, or forgotten. Whether this results from our own personal sin or demonic forces, we must guard and protect what the Spirit has given us.

Already in this chapter, we have seen scriptural teachings on unity in the church in Paul's letters to the Romans, Corinthians, Philippians, and Ephesians. We see a similar teaching in all of his other letters too. In fact, you can find teachings about love and unity within the body of believers in every single book in the New Testament. Other than the Lordship of Christ and fidelity to the gospel, love and unity among believers is one of the most consistently and frequently written exhortations, from Matthew through Revelation.

Some of these teachings fall in the final greetings sections of epistles, so it is easy to breeze past them. But in other books, we see the love and unity among believers set up as *the* sign confirming the truth of the gospel to the outside world (John 13:35). All that to say, it's a big deal.

Throughout history, sinful people have chosen division: division from God (since Adam and Eve) and division from each other (since Cain and Abel). The first and greatest commandment was broken by the first generation, and the second greatest commandment promptly broken by the second generation (Matthew 22:36–39). But we follow a God who traversed the separation between Him and sinful people by coming to earth in human form, tearing the curtain that set apart the holy of holies, destroying the dividing wall of hostility between people groups, and who will come again to be with His bride. He Himself is our peace (Ephesians 2:14).

Guarding the unity starts with recognizing the existence of our unity in Christ. Just as there is one God and Father of all, there is one church. There is one Spirit and one body. One Lord and one faith. One Bridegroom and one bride. Not multiple: "Jesus is coming back, and he's coming for a bride, not a harem."[27]

That Which Divides

Amid this talk of unity, we must remember that there are valid reasons for certain types of division, but there are a lot of caveats to that statement. For example, Jesus taught division, even division within families. In Matthew 10:34–36 (ESV), he said: "Do not think that I came to bring peace on earth. I did not come to bring peace but a sword. For I have come to 'set a man against his father, a daughter against her mother, and a daughter-in-law against her mother-in-law'; and 'a man's enemies will be those of his own household.'"

Paul also demonstrated division by leaving some groups (those who rejected Christ) to preferentially spend time with others who accepted Christ (Acts 19:9). But in both of these cases, what was the thing doing the dividing? Was it their personal cultural preferences or ideologies? No, it is the gospel itself that is the sword of division. The gospel is inherently divisive. To say that Christ is Lord is to simultaneously say no one else is Lord. To say Christ is the only way is to also say that all other ways are wrong. To say He is the Truth is to proclaim all others are false. That is divisive.

The real problem for us today is that it is not the gospel that is causing division, but other beliefs and opinions. Having strongly held opinions is fine, but for Christians today, we must learn how to attribute appropriate weight and prioritization to our beliefs. One way that I find helpful is to think in terms of concentric circles:[28]

The inner circle is *Christ Himself* as the Way, the Truth, and the Life. He is the absolute, nonnegotiable, nondebatable core of Christianity.

The next circle outside of that is Christian *dogma*, meaning the things that all Christians for all time have believed and agreed upon. This includes things such as God as Creator, the Virgin Birth, and the presence of the Holy Spirit. Basically, the contents of the Nicene Creed.

Outside of Christ the core and *dogma*, there lies *doctrine* in the next circle. These are the beliefs that distinguish different denominations (e.g., Baptist, Mennonite, Anglican), including believer's baptism versus infant baptism, the presence of female clergy or preachers, and the contents of a worship service.

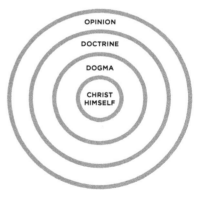

Beyond this, every other belief can be categorized as *opinion*—that is, everything else that doesn't fall into the previous circles.

The benefit of using these concentric circles is to distinguish appropriate weight and priority to our beliefs and what type of division is or isn't appropriate. The inner circles of Christ's Lordship and Christian *dogma* are what distinguish Christians from non-Christians. Christians agree and believe these inner circles are true; non-Christians do not. We still love and pray for those who do not believe like we do, and we work to point them to Christ, but they are not a member of the body of Christ.

Going out from there, you can see, once you reach the *doctrine* circle, good, Bible-believing, Jesus-loving Christians can disagree. This circle leads to the practical division of denominations. Christians across denominations are all unified in Christ, but our differing doctrinal convictions lead us to commune and worship and express devotion to our one Father in heaven in distinct ways. And that is OK!

On more than one occasion, I have had the privilege to worship and commune together with Mennonites, Anglicans, Baptists, nondenominational Christians, and Messianic Christians, as well as churches that were all white, Black, Hispanic, and many other ethnicities and languages. Some churches I've attended have priests wearing robes, and others have rock bands with smoke machines. Some serve grape juice for communion, and others have actual wine. I love the diversity within the body of Christ. But this diversity among local churches should not disrupt or threaten the unity among the "capital-C" global Church.

The final, outer circle is reserved for *opinions* about everything else. These are the beliefs we have that are furthest from the center of our concentric circles, meaning they should be our lowest priority relative to the other, more central and essential circles. This includes everything as trivial as sports team preferences to bigger issues such as beliefs about abortion. Residing in the realm of opinion does not mean it's not important. There are a lot of important issues that we can and should have strong convictions about. But as opposed to the previous circles, they should not threaten or be equated with the unity we have in Christ and should not be allowed to cause division among the people of God.

These circles help us see the relative importance of beliefs and determine if, when, and how division should or should not occur. If a pastor gets up on Sunday and says that he has decided that Jesus was not divine, that is a big deal. As the divinity of Jesus is a gospel-based, core issue, that warrants some (loving) division. If he gets up and says that he voted for the candidate you despise, you can talk about it later, but it should not be a point of division and disunity in the church.

We unify *around* Christ and Him alone, and we are unified *in* Christ and Him alone. To unify or preach unity around anything less, elevating it to a place only reserved for Christ, is heretical. We must guard our unity in Christ from calls to unify around things other than Christ. If we allow *doctrine* and *opinions* to divide us, we are elevating them in importance equal to or above Jesus Himself. If it is truly Jesus who unites us, the outer circles issues cannot divide us. In contrast, if the outer circle issues *do* divide us, we have failed to guard our unity in Christ.[29]

Back in the introduction, I mentioned friends who were previously in a Bible study together, but who were now disparaging each other based on their views about COVID. They were no longer speaking and had gone their separate ways. This is an example of an *opinion* that is given too much weight that has no right to threaten the unity in the church. Our bond is Christ, and that should be stronger than any opinion: "So in Christ Jesus you are all children of God through faith, for all of you who were baptized into Christ have clothed yourselves with Christ. There is neither Jew nor Gentile, neither slave nor free, nor is there male and female, for you are all one in Christ Jesus" (Galatians 3:26–28).

When Paul wrote this, he didn't mean that the Jews and Gentiles lost their cultural heritage or that men and women lost their defining physical characteristics. He was saying that, compared to our identity in Christ and our unity as one in Christ, all of these other things are of so much lesser importance that, in comparison, it might as well be like they were gone.

Gospel Deficiency makes us lose our sense of reality and priorities. The reality is that in Christ, we are all one. According to

Paul, now there is neither Republican nor Democrat, neither vaccinated nor unvaccinated, nor is there Presbyterian or Pentecostal. For we are all one in Christ Jesus. So if you are part of a certain denomination, fine. If you prefer to vote a certain way, go ahead. Once again, the focus here is on the gospel of Jesus Christ taking its proper place in our lives over and above everything other issue or categorization. When the King is truly on the throne of our lives, everything else falls into its proper place, far below the Lordship of Christ.

Chapter Nine
Remission

"Therefore, I urge you, brothers and sisters, in view of God's mercy, to offer your bodies as a living sacrifice, holy and pleasing to God—this is your true and proper worship. Do not conform to the pattern of this world, but be transformed by the renewing of your mind. Then you will be able to test and approve what God's will is—his good, pleasing and perfect will." (Romans 12:1–2)

With many medical issues, after you have a condition once, it often predisposes you to recurrence. People are most familiar with this concept as it relates to cancer, with references to being "in remission" in common parlance. But just because you reach remission does not mean the battle is over and you forget about it. If I have lung cancer from smoking my whole life and then enter remission after chemotherapy, that does not mean I can start smoking again. Maintaining remission takes work. It's the work of practicing a healthy lifestyle and monitoring for signs of recurrence.

Likewise, the condition of Gospel Deficiency, even after treatment, can easily return. Because of this, after addressing and treating the many facets of Gospel Deficiency, we must take proper steps to stay in remission and prevent recurrence. This comes in the form of renewing your mind daily to be the mind of Christ (remission) and prayerfully abiding in Christ (prevention). This is the focus of the present chapter and the one that follows.

A Slave No More

All humans are born into bondage and slavery to sin. Even if we are now following Christ and have been transformed into a righteous, reconciled, new creation, we were all at one point unbelievers blinded by Satan and unable to see the light of the gospel (2 Corinthians 4:4). That is the bondage we are born into. As Christians, our new reality is that the blood of Christ has freed us from slavery to sin and darkness and brought us into His everlasting light. Unfortunately, despite seeing and experiencing this new reality, our minds often revert back to old ways of thinking. We need to free our mind—or, more accurately, have our mind freed by the Spirit—to live into the fullness of this new life.

Billions of people around the world are living and dying every day in bondage and remain blinded to the gospel. But the Lord has made His light shine in us, and by this light we preach Christ and Him crucified to those blinded by the god of this age. For us to recognize this reality and the need of others, our minds must be free from our past way of thinking. Our minds must be freed and transformed to see the lost people around us as they truly are: captives to darkness in need of a Savior.

In terms of viewing other people through the lens of our Gospel Glasses, this is a war that is waged on the battlefield of the mind. Many of us habitually view others through the distorted lens of our sinful nature. If you don't think you do this, try to tune into your background thoughts next time you are out and about, and you will likely catch yourself doing it.

A mind conformed to the pattern of this world underlies every symptom of Gospel Deficiency that we have discussed. Therefore, treating this is a key to staying in remission. Paul gives us a prescription in Romans 12:1–2 in the form of his exhortation to be transformed by the renewing of your mind. Chapter 12 of Romans starts with "Therefore." As they say, if you see a "therefore," always ask what it's *there for*. In this case, Paul was using "therefore" to reference chapters 1–11 in which he expounded on and elucidated all that Christ has done for us. In 12:1, Paul introduced this section with, "in view of God's mercy." All of Romans up to this point can be summarized under the umbrella of the mercy of God in action.[30] That is the gospel. Therefore, this transition is his way of saying, "Because of everything I've been explaining so far, and because of everything God has done, here is what should happen next." Here at the start of chapter 12, Paul transitioned to examine how the gospel of Christ should affect our lives.

This application section of Romans describes the aspects and attributes of a gospel-centered life. Paul clearly believed that "the gospel unleashes God's power so that people, by embracing it, can be rescued from the disastrous effects of sin, being pronounced 'righteous' in God's sight and having a secure hope for salvation from wrath in the last day."[31] He looked back at what Christ had done while simultaneously looking forward to the eternal implications.

The letter continues with the exhortation to "offer your bodies as a living sacrifice." In Texas we would say, "Y'all offer y'all's bodies," to make it clear Paul wasn't talking to a singular person with multiple bodies. But why does God want us to offer a bodily sacrifice if Jesus already offered Himself as a single sacrifice for sins once and for all (Hebrews 10:12)? For starters, the gospel does not automatically produce obedience in our lives, unfortunately, but the Spirit within us can guide us toward the obedience that the gospel demands.

Second, our "bodies" that we are called to sacrifice are not specifically the physical body, like the Old Testament sacrifices that required the body and blood of an animal. Paul here was speaking metaphorically to imply that we should offer our entire selves, especially emphasizing our interaction with the world, which is made clear as chapter 12 of Romans progresses. Because the gospel does not turn us into Christ-like automatons, we must submit every aspect of our life, and specifically how we think about and relate to others, to the work of the Spirit.

Third, this offering is meant to be ongoing and repeated. Unlike Christ's sacrifice that was once and for all, we don't have the ability to make this a one-time deal. We are ever-changing, unsteady, fickle, and imperfect. Therefore, we must offer ourselves as a sacrifice every minute of every hour of every day. In this case, the New Revised Texas Version would read, "Y'all don't quit offering y'all's bodies, now, ya hear?"

Finally, in Romans 12:2 we get to Paul's prescription to avoid the recurrence or onset of Gospel Deficiency: "Do not conform to the pattern of this world, but be transformed by the renewing of your mind." A renewed mind comes from the work of the Holy Spirit. He alone knows the thoughts of God, and He alone gives us spiritual insight and understanding, which is far above all human wisdom and understanding. It is with this renewed mind that we are able to judge everything, and everyone, with the mind of Christ. As Paul said, "The person with the Spirit makes judgments about all things, but such a person is not subject to merely human judgments . . . But we have the mind of Christ" (1 Corinthians 2:15–16).

But wait a minute. I thought we weren't supposed to judge. You know, like, "Judge not lest ye be judged" and all that. (Side note: Isn't it funny how so many biblical commands about what not to do are remembered in their King James Version?) This is a case where two different words in the original text translate to the same English word. The "bad" judging that we think about in "Thou shalt not" terms refers to the act of assuming power over someone to critique or censor them. On the other hand, the "good" judgment that Paul told the Corinthians that all Spirit-filled people do refers more to a close examination or investigation in an effort to discern the truth. Basically, think reality TV competition for the first type and a true crime docuseries for the second type.

We have seen that Gospel Deficiency often manifests in how we view others, particularly viewing them apart from the gospel and in the light of the here and now rather than in the light of eternity. The prescription to treat this is to continually offer our lives and minds to be transformed and renewed by the Holy Spirit. In this we can live into the mind of Christ.

To take it one step further, "With a transformed and renewed mind under the control of the Spirit, it is impossible to be arrogant and self-centered."[32] Rather, our mind will focus on loving others and pointing them to Christ rather than viewing them as a means to love and highlight ourselves and our interests. The mind of Christ is unable to see others as anything less than beloved sons and daughters of our Father in heaven, who ascribed unsurpassable worth to them by dying for them on the cross. In humility and generosity, those guided by the mind of Christ will give freely to others what we have received freely from our Father in heaven—that is, His grace and love and good news of the kingdom.

The Holy Spirit is always at work in the hearts and minds of believers and unbelievers. For those of us who are followers of Christ, He is continually at work in us to mold us into greater degrees of godliness. Only He has the power to change hearts and renew minds, if we will let Him. Only He has the power to help us see people around us through Gospel Glasses, through the lens of the cross framed by eternity. Most of us know this, but there is a difference between knowing the gospel path and walking the gospel path. In this regard, the Holy Spirit can show us the door, but we are the ones who have to choose to walk through it.

Metacognition

As the Holy Spirit works to renew our minds, we may find our brain resisting change. The brain is actually hardwired to protect itself. At its core, it is a selfish organ that operates based on what is best for its own survival. Physiologically, when there is stress on the body such as illness or a lack of oxygen, blood and oxygen are preferentially shunted to preserve the brain as much as possible, even if that means sacrificing other organs such as the kidneys or liver. As the physical brain is the seat of the mind, this selfish nature complicates the problem of freeing our mind to be like the mind of Christ.

When it comes to interacting with the outside world, the mind or brain acts similarly. For example, the brain goes into physiologic, hormonal fight-or-flight mode when strongly held beliefs are challenged. The stress hormone cortisol is released, which can essentially shut down the rational part of the brain, thus preventing us from absorbing information and processing it rationally. Conversely, when we are exposed to information that reinforces our strongly held beliefs, our brain releases a surge of pleasure hormones that make us feel good. Because of this, we continue, knowingly or unknowingly, to seek out things and ideas that make us feel good. This leads to us seeking to reinforce our preexisting, strongly held beliefs over and over again. It becomes like a drug, and we can get addicted. And to protect this addiction, the brain becomes less and less likely to tolerate information that takes away that feeling.

The same is true of how we see people. Physiologically (not just psychologically), the brain reacts positively to people who make us feel good and negatively to people who make us feel bad. This is applicable to Gospel Deficiency because we tend to put people into boxes based on noneternal, nongospel attributes such as their profession or their opinions or the quality of their work. In doing this we are prone to categorize and equate people with their boxes rather than seeing them through Gospel Glasses as beloved sons and daughters of the Creator. For example, if we have a preferred news outlet or political party that tells us what we want to hear, our brains begin to associate those news anchors, politicians, and supporters with the pleasurable feeling, and therefore, in our minds they become "the good people." Likewise, when certain people espouse opinions or give news reports that go against our preexisting beliefs, our brains tend to reject that information, regardless of whether it is true, and will subsequently place those folks in the category of "the bad people." This same principle can be applied to your family and coworkers and anyone you encounter. Our brain will constantly categorize people as good or bad based on whether they make our brain feel good or bad.

You can see how this potentially undermines the work of the Holy Spirit in renewing our mind. He continually tries to help us see all people through Gospel Glasses as a beloved creation for whom Christ died while our brains see people through self-centered glasses. This is a battle that we have to fight every day. Hence, Paul exhorted us to *continually* renew our minds. The powers of darkness do not rest. Our brain doesn't sleep. With these working 24/7 to pull us back down into the muck of the depraved mind Paul mentions in Romans 1:28, we must remain vigilant and hold fast to the Holy Spirit, who transforms us toward Christ-likeness through the renewing of our mind.

Stay in Shape

The daily renewal of our mind is an uphill battle, especially with our own brain working against us in some ways. The Holy Spirit is the one doing the heavy lifting here, as He is the one working out our sanctification. But that doesn't mean we sit idly by and hope to wake up one morning all fresh and renewed and ready to go. There are simple exercises that we can do to retrain our brain and help this process along.

Exercise 1

Ask the Lord to bring to mind someone toward whom you have ill will or negative feelings. Maybe it is the neighbor who never mows their lawn, or the coworker who chews their food too loudly, or the person who broke your heart or is hateful toward you. Now, ask the Holy Spirit to help you don your Gospel Glasses, renew your mind, and get a glimpse of the way the Lord sees that person. This does not mean you don't see the ways they have wronged you, just as the Lord sees the ways we wrong Him. But with His eyes, you can begin to see that person as a beloved creation who is in need of a Savior, just like you, for whom the Spirit is working to draw closer to Himself with their eternal destiny in mind. If that person is not a follower of Christ, ask God to reveal their deep need of the gospel to you and pray that they would have the opportunity to hear and respond to the good news of Jesus Christ.

Exercise 2

Think of one of your most strongly held beliefs—something that you are very passionate about. Let's say, for example, you are a diehard, straight-ticket-voting, card-carrying member of a certain political party. In this case, you likely have a favored news station that tends to agree with your political views. For this exercise, next time you turn on the news, flip channels to the other station—you know, the one that is the favored outlet for the other political party. Now turn on that station, and amid hearing and seeing reports that may trigger your brain toward anger and rejection and stress, take a deep breath, put on your Gospel Glasses, and pray for the people who are triggering you. Pray that the news anchor disparaging your favorite politicians will come to know Christ. Ask the Lord to give you eyes to see them and any others you see from the opposition as beloved creations for whom Christ died. Push your mind to process what you see and hear through the filter of eternity and focus only on what has eternal significance. Then align your heart with our Father's heart to see His kingdom come and will be done on earth as it is in heaven. Finally, repent for any un-Christlike thoughts or reactions you have during the process, praying, "Lord Jesus Christ, son of God, have mercy on me, a sinner." You can pray this along with a simple breathing exercise: *breathe in*, "Lord Jesus Christ, son of God," and *breathe out*, "Have mercy on me, a sinner." As you daily pursue the renewal of your mind, this simple breath prayer can be repeated any time you feel your mind wander toward earthly things and away from the things above (Colossians 3:2).

Chapter Ten
Prevention

"He must become greater. I must become less." (John 3:30)

As the old saying goes, an ounce of prevention is worth a pound of cure. Perhaps you've made it this far without finding any evidence of Gospel Deficiency in your life. Or maybe you are undergoing treatment or in remission. Wherever you fall in relation to this illness, there are two key requirements to continue on your journey toward healing.

Prayer and reliance on the Holy Spirit have been common themes in the treatment sections of each chapter. But make no mistake, these are not merely means to an end. Prayer is not some over-the-counter treatment we purchase when we don't feel well. The Holy Spirit is not an urgent care clinic doctor we visit on the rare occasion we have a problem.

These are important foundational pieces that must be in place in our lives for us to stay connected to Him and to effectively fulfill the work to which He has called us. If we are going to lovingly submit to our Savior and show people what it means to follow Christ, we must be the kind of disciple whom God wants to multiply. So what does that look like? Here are two essentials that must be true of us as we go out into the world to point people to Christ and prevent the spread of Gospel Deficiency.

Chapter Ten

Abiding in Christ

In John 15:1–10, Jesus talked about what it means to abide in Him. This is essentially the foundation of the entire Christian life. In this passage, Jesus said very explicitly, "Apart from me you can do nothing." This being the prerequisite for everything else, it will do us well to take a deep dive into what it means to abide in Christ. We will do this by answering three questions. Note your answers to each question before reading the corresponding section.

In this passage, what are the key elements of abiding?

We don't use the word *abide* much in modern English language, but fortunately, this passage spells out pretty clearly what it means to abide in Christ. The first thing that jumps out is the need for closeness or attachment to Christ. As a branch is attached to the vine, we must be so close to Him that He is able to fill us with everything we need for life and fruit-bearing. The vine collects water and nutrients and passes it on to the branches. Likewise, we must get all our life, love, purpose, and filling from Him. The branch does nothing on its own. Its only job is to stay attached and let the vine work through it to bear fruit. We must remain in close relationship with Christ and surrender to His will as the branch surrenders to the will of the vine.

Next is the need for obedience. In verses 9–10, Jesus conflated obedience with abiding. He said, "Now abide in my love. If you keep my commands, you will abide in my love." The link between lovingly abiding in Christ and obeying His word is inseparable. The implication is that we cannot fully abide in Him if we do not obey His commands.

Finally, we see that we must trust God with the end result. Just as the vine purposes to bear fruit for the whole plant, God works through our lives to bear fruit for His glory. All the branch has to do is hold fast to the vine and trust that the fruit will come at the right time. Sometimes part of trusting God with the outcomes includes allowing Him to prune us. On the surface, pruning may appear destructive, but the Master Gardener knows what He is doing and how to maximize fruit production. Again, we must surrender to Him.

Why is abiding essential?

The essential need to abide in Christ is summed up in verse 5: apart from Him we can do nothing. No good fruit can come from our lives apart from Him. Without Him our lives might bear something, but it won't be the kind of fruit anyone wants to eat. In our Western culture, it is easy to let our independent, do-it-yourself mindset affect our walk with Christ and eventually push God out of our minds. We often end up following our own will and then asking God to bless it on the backend. A complete and utter reliance on Him for anything good in our lives goes to the core of what it means to be a follower of Christ.

What distracts us or impedes our abiding life?

After seeing the importance of abiding in Christ, the last question is: What is getting in the way and how do I remove it? We have already seen how self-reliance can impede our abiding in Christ, but many external distractors exist as well. In our culture, millions of things are vying for our attention every moment of every day. Recent studies estimate that the average American is exposed to thousands of advertisements each day. Add to that the constant flood of social media posts, text messages, emails, and news updates, and it is easy to see that there are a lot of potential distractions to our abiding life. Whatever it is, the important thing is to identify it and come up with a plan to limit it so that our abiding life can flourish unimpeded. Stop and seriously think through the specific things that impede your abiding in Christ, and ask the Lord to show you how to handle them.

People of Prayer

Prayer is not a means to an end. Prayer is not a tool to bolster your work or ministry. Prayer *is* ministry. Spending time with the Lord in prayer is an end unto itself. The New Testament church and its leaders were characterized by a fervent, radical commitment to prayer. They did not pursue any work or make any plans without first bathing it in prayer. The same should be true of us.

Identifying our Gospel Deficiency is not a call to a new strategy or a new way of doing ministry. It is a call to fall on our knees at the feet of our loving Savior and let Him remodel our lives. It is a call to seek the heart of Christ and join Him in his prayer: to plead with the Father that His kingdom would come so fully in our cities, neighborhoods, and people groups that it would be just like heaven. We need the Author of our salvation to reveal to us His will for our lives and to overwrite all of our gospel-deficient ways so that His will may be done in and through us.

One of the most prolific disciple-makers of our time, Ying Kai, started a disciple-making movement in China that, in ten years, saw over one million new baptized believers and over 150,000 churches planted. When asked how this was possible and what strategy or method led to this, he would point to two indentations in the wooden floor of his house. This is where his knees would rest for hours each day as he was praying, pleading with the Lord for His kingdom to come in China. Prayer is not a supplement to gospel work; prayer *is* the work.

At the end of his letter to the Colossians, Paul passed along greetings from Epaphras, who is credited with planting the Colossian church. Paul writes, "Epaphras, who is one of you and a servant of Christ Jesus, sends greetings. He is always wrestling in prayer for you" (Colossians 4:12). The word Paul used, translated as "wrestling," connotes straining and struggling with every muscle in the body as one would in warfare. Epaphras loved these people so much that he was constantly engaged in intense prayer for them. When was the last time we prayed like that for anyone?

As God breaks our heart for the lost people around us, it can be overwhelming to think about how many people are in desperate need of the gospel. Trying to wrap our mind around billions of people who are lost and headed for an eternity apart from God can be paralyzing. How can we even begin to make a dent in this huge need? On our own this is impossible. Paul and the early church recognized this. Ying Kai recognized this. And it drove them to their knees in desperation, pleading with the Lord to make a way to bring the gospel to a lost and dying world. God provided for them, and He continues to provide for those who seek Him and His heart for the world today.

A Firm Foundation

These two elements—abiding in Christ and praying in accordance with the Father's heart—are the foundation of the entire Christian life. This is the foundation on which everything else is built.

Nothing that truly reflects and honors God can come apart from these. For apart from Him we can do nothing. If this foundation is not in place, there is nothing on which to build.

Our Western culture loves to perform tasks, to work, to build, and to create. Therefore, we in the Western church love to do ministry and have programs and church services. But sometimes we can begin to love ministry and programs and church services more than we love Jesus. These foundational pieces stem from a love of God. We must be careful not to fall in love with serving God more than loving God Himself.

In 1 Corinthians 13:1–3 Paul talked about doing seemingly great, godly things without love and how this equates to nothing:

> If I speak in the tongues of men or of angels, but do not have love, I am only a resounding gong or a clanging cymbal. If I have the gift of prophecy and can fathom all mysteries and all knowledge, and if I have a faith that can move mountains, but do not have love, I am nothing. If I give all I possess to the poor and give over my body to hardship that I may boast, but do not have love, I gain nothing.

No matter what "great" work we do, if we aren't full of love for God and for people, then, as this verse says, in reality we do nothing, are nothing, and gain nothing. This verse could similarly be applied to us today. If I preach eloquently so that all can understand, but I do not have love, I'm just making noise. If I have the gift of knowledge and can teach all people what it means to follow Christ, but I do not have love, I am nothing. If I give all of my time and money and even my life to church programs or to further noble causes, but I do not have love, I gain nothing.

The only thing worth gaining in this life is the King and His kingdom. The Kingdom of God is the only thing on this earth worth possessing, even if we possess nothing else. If we possess everything else but do not welcome, possess, and experience the reality and presence of the Kingdom of God, we possess nothing of eternal significance.[33]

We must be filled with the love of God first and foremost. We demonstrate love for God by obeying His commands, including the command to make disciples (John 15:10). And we demonstrate that love for people by giving them the opportunity to hear and respond to the gospel (1 Thessalonians 2:8). Apart from Him we can do nothing, and without love, we and our ministry amount to nothing.

Practical

What are some practical ways to help you or your church prevent the spread of Gospel Deficiency?

Spread awareness

The first step is to recognize the problem. If we don't know it is an issue, we can't do anything to remedy it. Just like there is breast cancer awareness month, maybe your church should have a gospel awareness month to discern and evaluate the health of the congregation and diagnose any pernicious signs of Gospel Deficiency.

Screening

Most pastors admit that their church has a lot of room to grow in terms of evangelism and making new disciples. But how often and intentionally is this being evaluated? Perhaps an annual, a biannual, or a quarterly screening is in order so that if Gospel Deficiency does develop you can catch it early. A regularly scheduled series or Bible study focused on living into gospel sufficiency could foster a healthy gospel culture in your church community.

Loving accountability

Integrate loving accountability into your gatherings to help each other maintain an eternal, gospel-centered mindset. Give each other freedom to ask hard questions and point out skewed thinking in a loving way aimed at building each other up.

Chapter Eleven
Gospel Sufficiency

The room was quiet. No one was talking, but a million things were happening. Like one body with many parts, the medical team composed of nurses, respiratory therapists, pharmacists, and doctors all performed their individual tasks working toward one common task: save this life. Distinct yet unified. Separate but together. We worked. The tension in the air was palpable.

After several minutes of chest compressions, breathing assistance, targeted electrical shocks, and a cocktail of life-saving medications, the nurse exclaimed what we were all longing to hear. "He has a pulse!" An audible, combined sigh of relief emanated from the team. The patient's family, nervously and tearfully waiting in the hall, embraced me upon hearing the good news. The war wasn't over, but this battle was won.

There was still a lot of work to be done, but there was hope. The underlying cause was identified, treatment was underway, and we had a clear plan in place to keep this from happening again. It wasn't a simple recovery, but it was a recovery, and that's what matters most.

Once the acute, life-threatening sequelae of his previously undiagnosed, untreated, underlying diabetes resolved, we were able to determine his maintenance insulin therapy needs to replace his deficiency. This involved fine-tuning the amount and frequency of insulin he should inject each day as well as how and when to monitor his blood sugar levels. A substantial amount of time was also invested in diabetic education to ensure that he and his family understood his condition (i.e., what causes diabetes and how it affects your life), learned healthy lifestyle choices to keep it under control, understood how to use his resources (e.g., blood glucose monitor, testing strips, insulin needles), and so on.

Nearly two weeks after his *code stat*, the newly diagnosed diabetic was discharged from the hospital. Every patient gets discharged, but for the few minutes his heart stopped, it wasn't certain whether he would leave through the front door or the back. This was a happy ending to a story that doesn't always end positively.

The root issue for this patient is that his body required something that it could not produce on its own. He needed regular monitoring and treatment from outside of himself to sustain his life. Without a diagnosis and proper treatment, he could not go on.

My hope for this book is to help diagnose and treat what has, for so long, gone undiagnosed and untreated in the American church. As with diabetes, Gospel Deficiency is a serious condition that is harmful and deadly to the spirit and is an underlying cause for a plethora of debilitating symptoms within the contemporary church.

The diabetic cannot produce insulin, so the doctor provides the replacement to sustain his life. Likewise, all people require the gospel. We cannot produce the hope and salvation of the gospel on our own. We cannot faithfully follow our heavenly Father without the life-changing effects of the gospel in our heart and mind. We cannot lead others to spiritual health without the one true treatment they lack. Therefore, we must go to the Great Physician daily. He alone can fill the gospel-shaped hole in our lives so that we can then refer others to Him as well.

When we step out into the world, we realize we are merely dying people speaking to other dying people. We are beggars pointing other beggars to bread. The only difference is, for those of us in Christ, we know where to find the cure. There will always be those who deny the efficacy of this treatment and who stir up opposition. We can't change that. All we can do is ask the Lord to give us this day our daily meds, lead us not into temptation toward worldly gospel-deficient fixes, and deliver us from evil.

Addressing Gospel Deficiency is more than just a prescription to "share the gospel more." This is about how we see everything and everyone around us in all situations through the lens of the cross. If we always had gospel vision, we would approach life in light of eternity and approach people with their eternal destiny at the forefront of our mind. We settle for, "Have a blessed day," when we should be asking, "Are they going to have a blessed eternity?" We settle for a vague abstract desire for being "a light" to those around us when we should be thinking about how to concretely combat the darkness in which these individuals are living and dying. That can only be done with the gospel. We preach Christ and Him crucified.

Spiritual Triage

In medicine, we constantly have to perform triage. This means assessing all the needs around us and then prioritizing where to work, moving from most to least urgent. The same must be true of Christians. We see a lot of problems and a lot of needs, but we rarely stop to spiritually triage. This leads to much time and energy and money spent on less urgent and sometimes even futile needs. We have to start triaging for eternity. We must stop prioritizing fixing worldly, temporal issues and neglecting the eternal, spiritual needs of the people around us.

The core, underlying root cause of Gospel Deficiency specifically and worldly living in general is separation from God. Sin separates us from God, and separation from God predisposes us to sin. It's a vicious, deadly cycle. For Christians and non-Christians alike, our chronic need for Christ is our terminal condition, and without Him we are incurable.

The most devastating imbalance in the world today is the unequal distribution, not of material resources, but of the light of the knowledge of God in Jesus Christ.[34] The underlying disease of a fallen world is that they don't know the Savior. They too have a Gospel Deficiency, but in their case they may have never heard it or seen it or experienced it. Those living lives of gospel sufficiency can offer the cure to those far from God. After all, for those living in sin, whatever their sin is, is merely a symptom, not the underlying disease. The cure to this disease is the good news. In light of this, Christians really have no right to keep the good news to themselves.

The gospel is enough. Christ is enough. He is the only cure for what ails our society. When we live into gospel sufficiency, we take a gospel-first approach to the world to introduce others to their Savior and demonstrate His love for them. We let the gospel provide the lens through which we see life and let that be enough. We resolve to know Christ and Him crucified and nothing less.

As Charles Spurgeon said, "If sinners be damned, at least let them leap to Hell over our dead bodies. And if they perish, let them perish with our arms wrapped about their knees, imploring them to stay. If Hell must be filled, let it be filled in the teeth of our exertions, and let not one go unwarned and unprayed for."[35]

What would it look like to commit to fighting tooth and nail to save the lost? What would it look like to say, "Over my dead body"? To sacrifice and fight and struggle to persuade them to turn away from that road and toward Christ? We cannot save them or change their heart ourselves. Only God can do that. But we can lovingly appeal to them relentlessly so that even one might be saved. We can give all we have so that not a single one goes unwarned and unprayed for.

Every day we encounter people who are drowning apart from Christ. But we know a life preserver is within reach. All we have to do is show them the way. If someone was actually drowning in a case like this, we wouldn't hesitate to point them to safety or call for help or even dive in ourselves. The threat of death and the need for a Savior are no less real for those living and dying without the gospel than if they were literally drowning. We cannot be content to stand by and watch it happen. We must muster the courage to point them to their eternal life preserver. To call for help, when needed. To dive in ourselves. Whatever it takes so that some may be saved. The waters may be treacherous and the outcome unknown, but sacrificing momentary comfort is a small price to pay to help others find eternal salvation.

Endnotes

Notes to Chapter 1

1. *Sherlock Holmes: A Game of Shadows*, directed by Guy Ritchie (Burbank, CA: Warner Brothers, 2011).

2. David E. Garland, "2 Corinthians," in *The New American Commentary* 29 (Nashville: Broadman & Holman Publishers, 1999), 30.

Notes to Chapter 2

3. "Openness to Jesus Isn't the Problem—the Church Is," Barna Access, accessed June 9, 2023, https://barna.gloo.us/articles/spiritually-open-issue-3.

4. In common parlance this political block is often referred to as "evangelicals." It turns out this label is quite ironic. The root of the word *evangelical* comes from the Greek for "good news," but from the outside this group is often characterized with bad news about the things they are against.

5. David experienced some anxiety about his enemies. Psalm 139:19–22 are as follows:

> If only you, God, would slay the wicked!
> Away from me, you who are bloodthirsty!
> They speak of you with evil intent;
> your adversaries misuse your name.
> Do I not hate those who hate you, Lord,
> and abhor those who are in rebellion against you?
> I have nothing but hatred for them;
> I count them my enemies.

Based on our discussion of loving our enemies and seeking reconciliation over condemnation, as well as using Psalm 139:23–24, these verses make it a bit awkward. How can we talk about loving our enemies and seeking reconciliation while quoting from a passage where David, a man after God's own heart, was bragging about hating his enemies and asking God to slay them?

This passage is often cross-referenced (the little letters in some Bibles that denote their relationship to other verses) with Matthew 5:43 where, Jesus said, "You have heard that it was said, 'Love your neighbor and hate your enemy.'" The "hate your enemy" part is the sentiment David was expressing here. In fact, Jesus used the same Greek word for "hate" as the Septuagint (Greek Old Testament) uses for "hate" in this Psalm. But we get clarification from the next verse, Matthew 5:44: "But I tell you, love your enemies and pray for those who persecute you." We see that Jesus is taking this very sentiment from the Old Testament that David was bragging about and flipping it on its head to give his followers a new way of living.

So when David, immediately after expressing his hatred for enemies, asked the Lord to search him and find any offensive way in him, we can imagine Jesus coming up to him: "Yeah . . . about that, David. Um . . . there actually *is* an offensive way in you, and you just wrote it down. I appreciate your passion for my name, but I actually want you to love your enemies and pray for them, so . . ." He is still doing the same thing for us today if we will listen.

6. Here I am referring to anxiety in the general sense of having anxious thoughts or worry. This is not referring to the clinical diagnosis of generalized anxiety disorder or related diagnoses that have an internal, physiological cause.

Notes to Chapter 3

7. This story is based on case reports and is not describing one of my actual patients. Just to be clear, I am not violating HIPAA.

8. Timothy Keller, *Counterfeit Gods: The Empty Promises of Money, Sex and Power, and the Only Hope that Matters* (New York: Penguin, 2009), xix.

9. Full disclosure, this was spoken by one of Job's misguided friends, Elihu, but it's too good of an analogy to pass up.

10. Written by Charlie Hall. © Copyright 2000.

Notes to Chapter 4

11. Author: Helen Howarth Lemmel (1922).

12. Quote adapted from David J. Hesselgrave, "The Eclipse of the Eternal in Contemporary Missiology," *The Journal of Evangelism and Missions: Beyond Conflict to Church Growth* 7 (2008): 58.

13. Christopher R. Little, *Polemic Missiology for the 21st Century: In Memoriam of Roland Allen* (Seattle: Amazon Kindle, 2011).

14. Oswald Chambers, "Vital Intercession," My Utmost for His Highest, accessed February 6, 2024, https://utmost.org/vital-intercession/.

Notes to Chapter 5

15. Garland, "2 Corinthians," 212.

16. Accomplishing something hard doesn't count. Sure, God may have helped you in your certain case, but it's not as if Christians have a monopoly on doing hard things.

17. Gordon D. Fee, *Paul, the Spirit, and the People of God* (Grand Rapids, MI: Baker, 1994), 18.

18. Don Dent, *The Ongoing Role of Apostles in Missions: The Forgotten Foundation* (Bloomington, IN: WestBow Press, 2019).

Notes to Chapter 6

19. *Reviving Evangelism: Current Realities That Demand a New Vision for Sharing Faith* (Ventura, CA: Barna Group, 2019).

20. Ibid.

21. Barna, "Openness to Jesus Isn't the Problem—the Church Is," *Spiritually Open*, May 1, 2023, https://barna.gloo.us/login?returnTo=%2Fspiritually-open.

22. *Reviving Evangelism.*

23. Douglas J. Moo, *The Letter to the Romans*, ed. Ned B. Stonehouse et al., 2nd ed., *The New International Commentary on the New Testament* (Grand Rapids, MI: Eerdmans, 2018), 763.

24. Robert E. Coleman, The *Master Plan of Evangelism*, repackaged ed. (Grand Rapids, MI: Revell, 2006).

Notes to Chapter 7

25. Mark I. Bubeck, *The Adversary* (Chicago: Moody Publishers, 2013), Kindle loc. 262.

Notes to Chapter 8

26. Of note, no one said a word about removing the Christian flag.

27. Shane Claiborne, *Irresistible Revolution: Living as an Ordinary Radical* (New York: Harper Collins, 2006), 145.

28. Credit to Greg Boyd for this analogy.

29. To be clear, there is a difference between unity and agreement. Unity is inherent in the body of believers and something we are called to guard. It is spiritual and eternal. Agreement just means that you think similarly about something. If you want to hang out and talk with people you agree with, great. Go for it. But as soon as you begin to feel unified in the biblical sense with those Christians to the exclusion of other Christians who disagree, you've gone too far.

Notes to Chapter 9

30. Douglas J. Moo, "The Letter to the Romans," in *The New International Commentary on the New Testament*, ed. Ned B.

Stonehouse et al., 2nd ed. (Grand Rapids, MI: Eerdmans, 2018), 768.

31. Moo, "The Letter to the Romans," 763.

32. Grant R. Osborne, "Romans: Verse by Verse," in *Osborne New Testament Commentaries* (Bellingham, WA: Lexham Press, 2017), 383.

Notes to Chapter 10

33. Tom Casey, *Studies in the Kingdom of God* (self-pub., 2017).

Notes to Chapter 11

34. Casey, *Studies in the Kingdom of God*.

35 Charles Spurgeon, "The Wailing of Risca," The Spurgeon Center, accessed February 6, 2024, https://www.spurgeon.org/resource-library/sermons/the-wailing-of-risca/#flipbook/.

SCAN HERE to learn more about Invite Press, a premier publishing imprint created to invite people to a deeper faith and living relationship with Jesus Christ.